SMP interact C1

Practice for Book C1

Contents

CAMBRIDGE
UNIVERSITY PRESS

PUBLISHED BY THE PRESS SYNDICATE OF THE UNIVERSITY OF CAMBRIDGE
The Pitt Building, Trumpington Street, Cambridge, United Kingdom

CAMBRIDGE UNIVERSITY PRESS
The Edinburgh Building, Cambridge CB2 2RU, UK
40 West 20th Street, New York, NY 10011–4211, USA
10 Stamford Road, Oakleigh, Melbourne 3166, Australia
Ruiz de Alarcón 13, 28014 Madrid, Spain
Dock House, The Waterfront, Cape Town 8001, South Africa

http://www.cambridge.org

First published 2001

Printed in the United Kingdom at the University Press, Cambridge

Typeface Minion   *System* QuarkXPress®

A catalogue record for this book is available from the British Library

ISBN 0 521 79866 3 paperback

Typesetting and technical illustrations by The School Mathematics Project
Cover design by Angela Ashton

3 Chance

Sections D, E and F

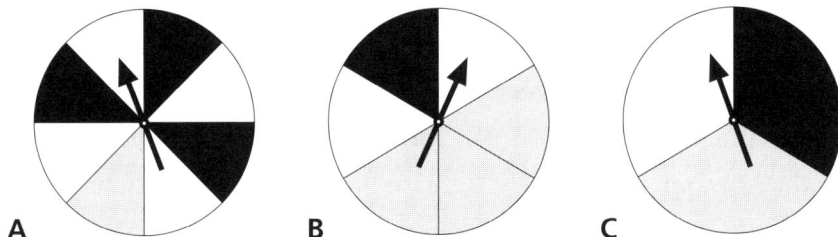

A   B   C

1 For each spinner, what is the probability that
    (a) white will win   (b) black will win
    (c) grey will win   (d) black will not win

2 You have decided to bet that
    (a) white will win   (b) black will win   (c) grey will win
    Which spinner would you choose in each case?

3 Write down three fractions equivalent to
    (a) $\frac{1}{4}$ (b) $\frac{3}{5}$ (c) $\frac{5}{8}$ (d) $\frac{4}{7}$

4 Simplify each of these fractions as far as possible.
    (a) $\frac{4}{8}$ (b) $\frac{8}{12}$ (c) $\frac{9}{15}$ (d) $\frac{16}{24}$ (e) $\frac{35}{60}$

5 One fraction in each set is not equivalent to the others. Which one?
    (a) $\frac{3}{6}$ $\frac{15}{30}$ $\frac{25}{55}$ $\frac{9}{18}$
    (b) $\frac{9}{15}$ $\frac{4}{6}$ $\frac{30}{45}$ $\frac{22}{33}$
    (c) $\frac{35}{50}$ $\frac{8}{10}$ $\frac{40}{50}$ $\frac{88}{110}$

6 Some of these fractions can be simplified.
    Simplify those that can as far as possible.
    (a) $\frac{24}{36}$ (b) $\frac{12}{35}$ (c) $\frac{30}{140}$ (d) $\frac{8}{54}$

7 Imagine these cards are turned over and shuffled around when you are not looking.

You choose a card at random.

| 1 | 4 | 4 | 6 | 9 | 24 | 27 | 36 | 81 |

What is the probability you will choose a card with

(a) the number 4   (b) the number 6   (c) a square number

(d) a multiple of 3   (e) a number greater than 25

(f) a two-digit number

8 Ann likes orange (**O**) sweets but not yellow (**Y**) ones.
She can pick a sweet at random from either bag A or B.
From which bag should she pick?
Why?

9 Rick likes blue (**B**) sweets, but not yellow (**Y**) or green (**G**) ones.
He can pick a sweet at random from bag P, Q or R.
From which bag should he pick?
Why?

If Rick liked yellow sweets as well as blue,
from which bag should he pick?

Section G

1 Two ordinary dice are rolled.

> The maximum when
> 3 and 5 are thrown is 5.

(a) Copy and complete this table showing the maximum of the two numbers. (If both numbers are 3, then the maximum is 3.)

(b) What is the most likely value of the maximum?

(c) What is the probability of this value?

Dice 2

1 2 3 4 5 6
Dice 1

2 A   B   C

Spinners A and B are spun.

Each square in this diagram shows a possible outcome. The shaded squares show the outcomes where A has the higher score.

What is the probability that A has the higher score?

Spinner B

3 4 8
Spinner A

3 Spinners B and C are spun.

What is the probability that B has the higher score?

4 Spinners A and C are spun.

What is the probability that C has the higher score?

*5 Two players choose a spinner each.
(They can't both choose the same one.)

If you were one of the players, would you prefer to choose your spinner first, or last? Why?

*6 If three people play with a spinner each, what is the probability that

(a) spinner A wins   (b) spinner B wins   (c) spinner C wins

4 Symmetry

Sections A and B

1 Which of these designs have rotation symmetry (of order greater than 1)?

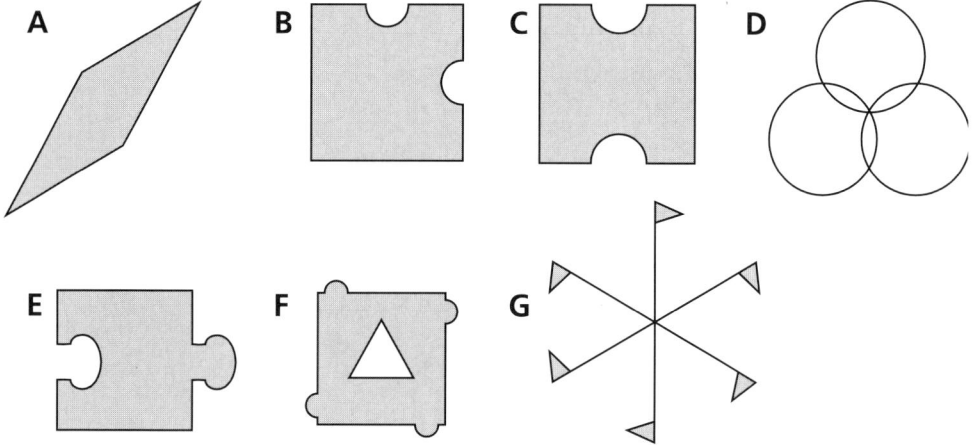

A

B

C

D

E

F

G

2 For each design, find the order of rotation symmetry.

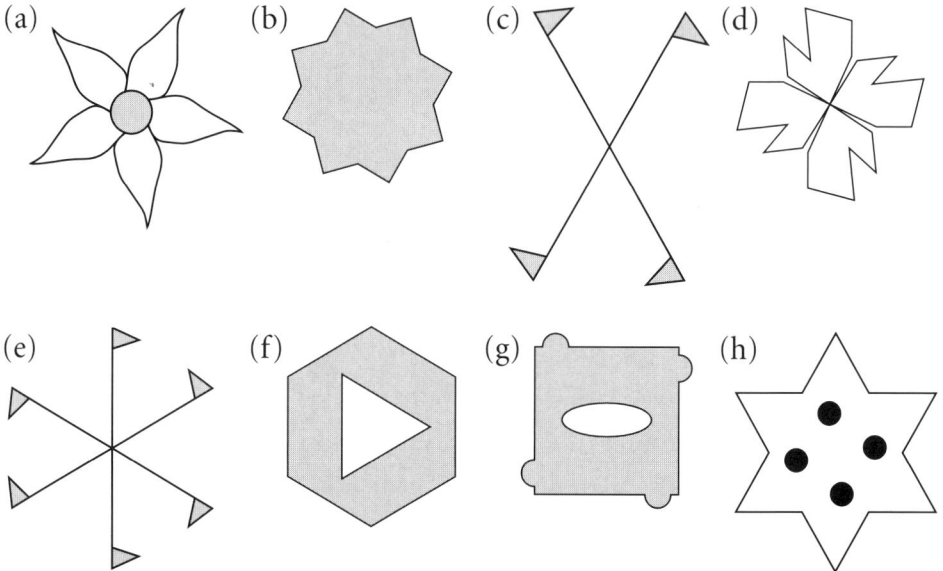

(a)

(b)

(c)

(d)

(e)

(f)

(g)

(h)

Section C

1 Copy and complete each design so it has rotation symmetry of order 4. Each centre is shown by a large dot.

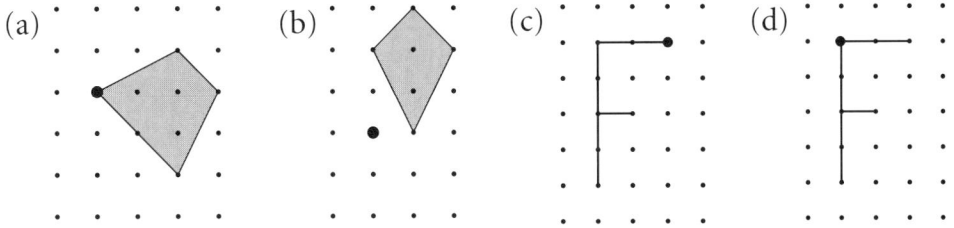

(a)

(b)

(c)

(d)

2 Copy and complete each design so it has rotation symmetry of order 2. Each centre is shown by a large dot.

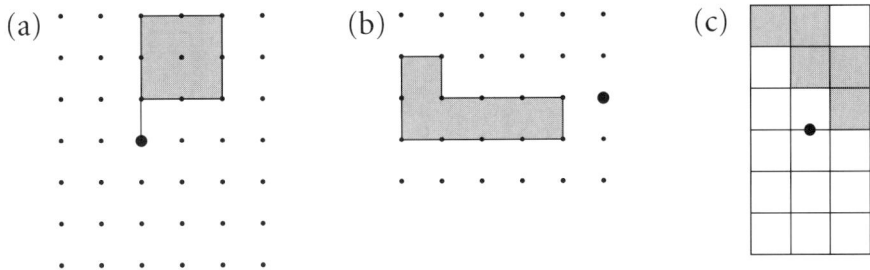

(a)

(b)

(c)

3 Copy and complete each design so it has rotation symmetry of order 3. Each centre is shown by a large dot.

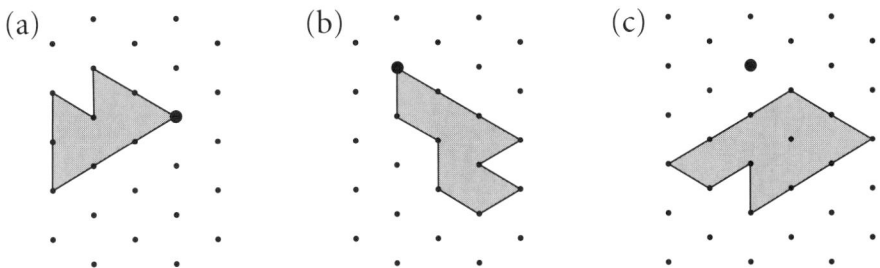

(a)

(b)

(c)

Sections D and E

1 Many of the walls of the Alhambra Palace in Spain are covered with tiling patterns. The diagrams below show some of these tiles.

Describe the symmetries of each tile.
(For example, 'The tile has no lines of symmetry. It has rotation symmetry of order 2.')

(a)

(b)

(c)

(d)

(e)

(f)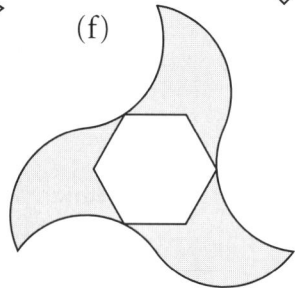

2 Describe the symmetries of each domino or card.

(a)

(b)

(c)

(d)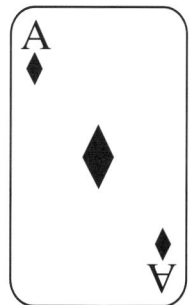

3 The diagrams show the shapes of some pieces from a computer game called 'Tetris'.

(a) Copy the diagrams.

Describe the symmetries of each piece.
Mark any centres of rotation and show all lines of symmetry.

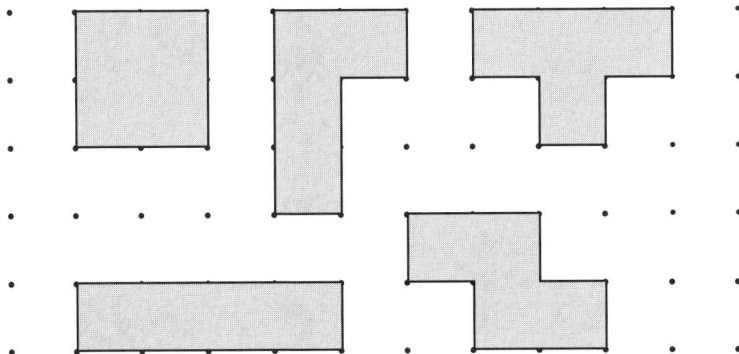

(b) This shape is made from two T-shaped pieces.
They do not overlap.

Describe the symmetries of this new shape.

(c) Use two T-shapes with no overlapping to make
    (i) a shape with rotation symmetry and no reflection symmetry
    (ii) a shape with rotation symmetry and reflection symmetry

(d) Choose one of the other Tetris pieces.
With two or more of your shapes, try to make a design with
    (i) reflection symmetry but no rotation symmetry
    (ii) reflection symmetry and rotation symmetry
    (iii) rotation symmetry of order 4

Sections F and G

This is part of an infinite pattern.

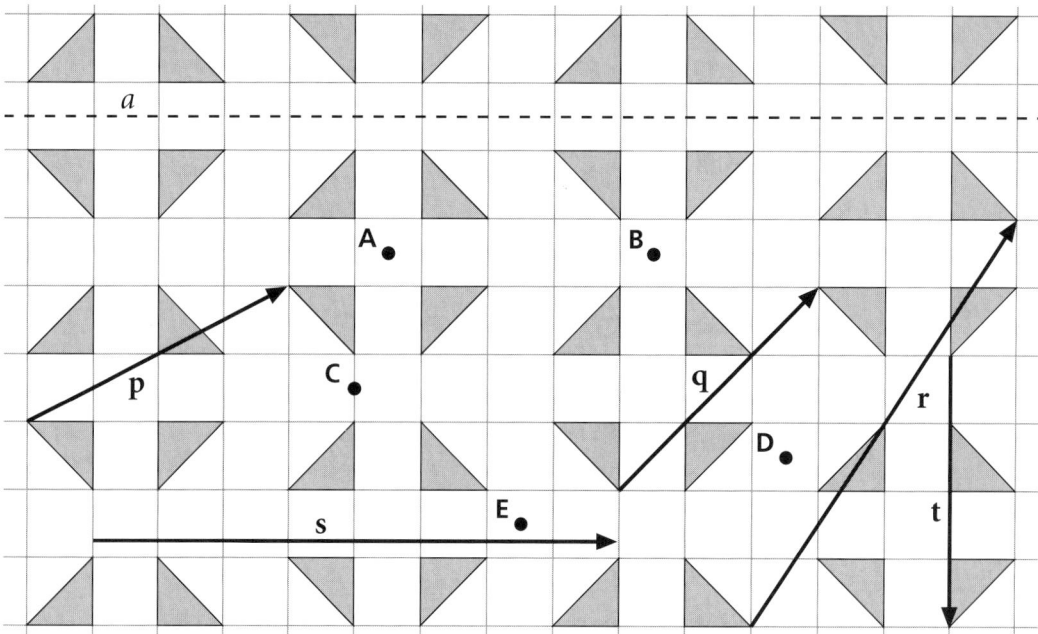

1   The horizontal line labelled *a* is a line of symmetry of the infinite pattern. How many other horizontal lines of symmetry can be drawn on the part of the pattern shown above?

2   How many vertical lines of symmetry can be drawn on the part of the pattern above?

3   Does the pattern have any diagonal lines of symmetry (╲ or ╱)? If so, how many can be drawn on the part of the pattern above?

4   Which of the points A, B, C, D, E are centres of rotation symmetry of the infinite pattern? Write down the order of symmetry for each centre.

5   If a tracing of the infinite pattern is translated as shown by arrow **p**, it will fit the pattern again. Describe the translation **p**.

6   Which of the arrows **q**, **r**, **s**, **t** show a translation that will make a tracing fit the pattern again?

5 Multiples and factors

Sections B, C and D

1 Goldbach's conjecture says that every even number greater than 4
can be expressed as the sum of two prime numbers.

For example, $10 = 3 + 7$ $20 = 7 + 13$ $100 = 47 + 53$

Find all the ways of expressing these as the sum of two primes.

(a) 30   (b) 100

2 Make factor trees for (a) 36   (b) 70

3 What are the missing numbers in these factor trees.

(a)

(b)

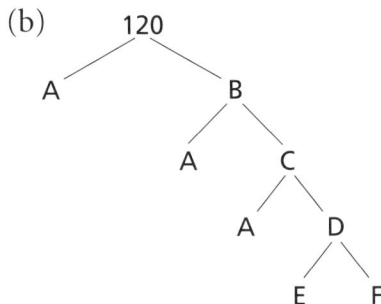

4 (a) Find the prime factorisation of 60.

(b) Use your aswer to (a) to find the prime factorisation of 600.

5 Find the prime factorisation of 14 400.

6 Find the missing numbers in these prime factorisations.

(a) $360 = 2^a \times 3^b \times 5$ (b) $756 = 2^a \times 3^b \times c$

7 Find the prime factorisation of each of these square numbers.

(a) 16 (b) 36 (c) 100 (d) 900

(e) What can you say about the powers in the prime factorisation
of a square number?

8 Here are some ways of arranging nine different digits so a correct multiplication occurs.

$12 \times 483 = 5796$ $\qquad$ $42 \times 138 = 5796$ $\qquad$ $18 \times 297 = 5346$

$27 \times 198 = 5346$ $\qquad$ $48 \times 159 = 7632$

Use these to find the prime factorisation of

(a) 5796 $\qquad\qquad$ (b) 5346 $\qquad\qquad$ (c) 7632

Sections E, F, G and I

1 Find the lowest common multiple (LCM) of

(a) 6, 12 and 15 $\qquad\qquad$ (b) 12 and 28

2 Write down the LCM of

(a) $2^2 \times 3$ and $3^3 \times 2$ $\qquad\qquad$ (b) $2 \times 3^2 \times 5$ and $2^3 \times 5$

(c) $3^2 \times 7$, 5×7^2 and 2×5^2 $\qquad\qquad$ (d) 3^4, $2^2 \times 3$ and 2×5^2

3 Find the highest common factor (HCF) of 48 and 72.

4 Write down the HCF of

(a) $2^2 \times 3$ and $3^3 \times 2$ $\qquad\qquad$ (b) $2 \times 3^2 \times 5$ and $2^3 \times 5$

(c) $3^3 \times 7$, $3^2 \times 7^2$ and $3^2 \times 7^3$ $\qquad\qquad$ (d) $2^4 \times 5^2$, and $2^2 \times 5^4$ and $2^3 \times 5^3$

5 Find the HCF of 506 and 1863.

6 Three bells ring at intervals of 18, 24 and 32 minutes.

If they all ring together at noon, when will they next all ring at the same time?

7 Four barrels can hold 72, 24, 56 and 120 litres.

What is the size of the biggest jug which can be used to fill them exactly?

8 A 'palindromic number' is one which reads the same when the order of its digits is reversed, e.g. 272 or 37873.

Which of these palindromic numbers are also prime?

101 $\qquad$ 111 $\qquad$ 121 $\qquad$ 131 $\qquad$ 141 $\qquad$ 151

⑥ Number grids

Sections A and B

1 (a) Copy and complete these number grids.
   (b) What is the diagonal rule for each grid?

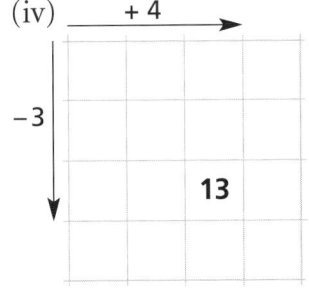

(i)
$$\xrightarrow{+5}$$
-2 | 7 | | |

(ii)
$$\xrightarrow{+3}$$
-2 | 7 | | |

(iii)
$$\xrightarrow{+2}$$
$+6$ | | 15 | |

(iv)
$$\xrightarrow{+4}$$
-3 | | | 13 |

2 Find the missing rule for each of these grids.

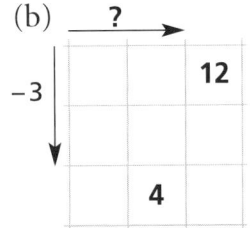

(a)
$$\xrightarrow{-4}$$
$?$ | | 6 | | 28 |

(b)
$$\xrightarrow{?}$$
-3 | | | 12 | | 4 |

Section C

1 (a) Copy and complete each of these grids.
   (b) For each grid, work out the number in the bottom right square when the number in the top left is 100.
   (c) For each grid, what number in the top left square would give 100 in the bottom right square?

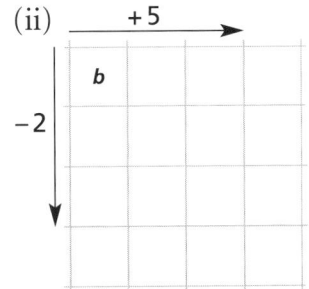

(i)
$$\xrightarrow{+4}$$
$+6$ | a | $a+4$ | |

(ii)
$$\xrightarrow{+5}$$
-2 | b | | |

2 Find the rules for each of these grids.

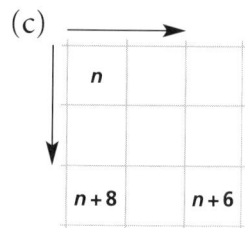

(a)

k	$k+3$	
	$k+11$	

(b)

	m	$m+10$
	$m+11$	

(c)

	n	
	$n+8$	$n+6$

3 Write each of these in a simpler way.

(a) $t+5+6$

(b) $a+3+4$

(c) $q+5+1$

(d) $p+1+2+1$

(e) $x+2+4+4$

(f) $y+5-3$

(g) $s-2-2$

(h) $v-1-3-1$

(i) $b-3+9$

(j) $a+3-7$

(k) $f-7-9$

(l) $c-5+12-5$

(m) $d-6+1-6$

(n) $g+3-4+3-4$

(o) $h-2-5-2-5$

Sections D, E and F

This chain of numbers is made using the rules '+ 2' and '+ 3'.

The two rules on top are the same.

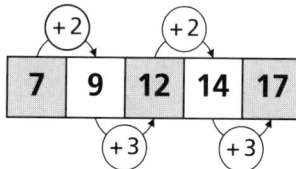

7	9	12	14	17

The two rules on the bottom are the same.

1 Copy and complete these chains.

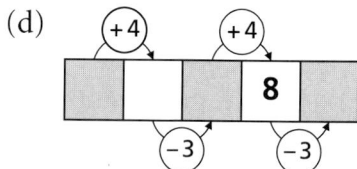

(a)

3				

(b)

			18	

(c)

		9		

(d)

			8	

14

2 Find the missing rule in each of these.

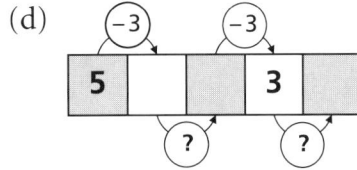

(a)

+4   +4
6   22
?   ?

(b)
?   ?
7   31
+5   +5

(c)
+5   +5
8   29
?   ?

(d)
−3   −3
5   3
?   ?

3 Find three different pairs of rules for this chain.

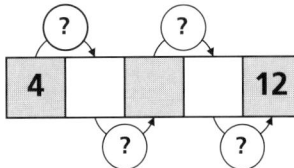

?   ?
4   12
?   ?

4 These chains are all made using the rules '+ 5' and '+ 2'.
For each chain, to find the ends total you add the first and last number.

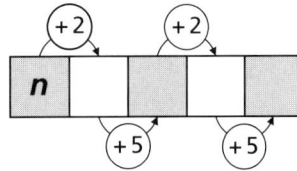

+2   +2
3   5   10   12   17
+5   +5

The ends total for this chain is 3 + 17 = 20.

+2   +2
4
+5   +5

+2   +2
5   19
+5   +5

+2   +2
n
+5   +5

(a) Copy and complete the chains.

(b) Copy and complete the ends total table.

(c) If the first number is 8, what is the ends total?

First number	Ends total
3	20
4	
5	
n	

5 Investigate other chains using your own pairs of rules.
Try to use algebra to explain your conclusions.

6 Find three pairs of equivalent expressions.

A $3a + 5$ **B** $2 + a - 6$ **C** $a + 4 + a - 5$

D $a + 2 + a + 3 + a$ **E** $2a - 6$ **F** $6a$

G $a - 2 + a - 4$ **H** $3 + a - 5$ **I** $2a - 1$

7 Write each of these in a simpler way.

(a) $p + p + 3$ (b) $y + 9 + y + y$ (c) $q + 8 + q + 2$

(d) $t + t + 5 - 2$ (e) $x + 6 + x - 4$ (f) $r + r - 2 + 8 + r$

(g) $w + w - 5 - 8$ (h) $j + j + 7 - 10$ (i) $h - 9 + h + 3$

8 These grids use the rules '+ 3' and '+ 2'.

$+3 \rightarrow$

$+2 \downarrow$

2	5	8
4	7	10
6	9	12

$+3 \rightarrow$

$+2 \downarrow$

3	6	9
5	8	11
7	10	13

$+3 \rightarrow$

$+2 \downarrow$

4	7	10
6	9	12
8	11	14

(a) You can find the grid total for each one by adding all the numbers in the grid. Copy and complete the grid total table.

(b) For these grids, find a rule that links the grid total to the top left number.

(c) What would the grid total be when the number in the top left is 50?

Top left	Grid total
2	63
3	
4	

9 Investigate grid totals for other sets of grids using your own pairs of rules. Try to use algebra to explain your conclusions.

10 Simplify these expressions where possible.

(a) $3n \times 2n$ (b) $5p \times 7$ (c) $2 + 4m - 5$

(d) $12q - 2$ (e) $a \times 3a$ (f) $4s - 3 - 3s + 8$

⑦ Constructions

Section C

1   Draw a line *l* and mark a point A on it.
Use ruler and compasses to construct a line through A
perpendicular to *l*.

Use ruler and compasses to bisect one of the right angles.
(This is the construction for an angle of 45°.)

2   Draw a line *l* and mark a point A on it.

Draw an arc, centred at A,
cutting the line *l* at B.

Do not alter the radius.
Draw an arc, centred at B,
to cross the first arc at C.

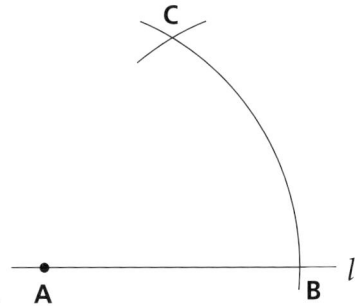

(a) What is the size of angle CAB?

(b) Bisect angle CAB using ruler and compasses.

3   Draw a circle (radius about 5 to 6 cm).

Draw any three lines forming a
triangle inside the circle, like this.

Mark a point P on the circle.

Use ruler and compasses to construct
the line from P perpendicular to one
of the three lines.

Mark the point A where it cuts the line.

Do the same for each of the other two lines,
marking points B and C.

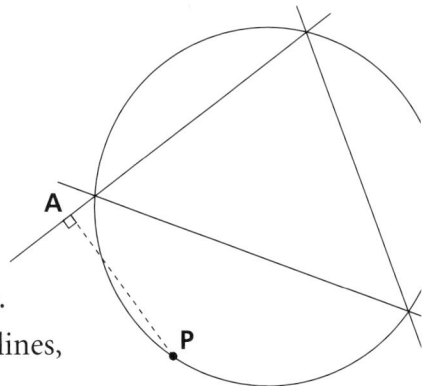

What do you notice about the points A, B and C?

⑧ Comparisons

Sections A, B and C

1   These dot plots show the weights of some litters of puppies.
    For each one, find the median weight of the puppies.

   (a) Dalmatians

   (b) Golden retrievers

   (c) Labradors

2   On graph paper, draw a number line from 110 to 150.

   (a) Draw a dot plot for the weights of these puppies.

   120 g   142 g   118 g   135 g   145 g   129 g

   (b) What is the median weight of the puppies?

3   Here are the temperatures one week in Barcelona and in Birmingham.

   Barcelona   21°C   22°C   19°C   26°C   30°C   21°C   18°C
   Birmingham   17°C   22°C   23°C   21°C   25°C   25°C   21°C

   (a) What is the median temperature in each city?

   (b) Which city has the higher median temperature that week?

   (c) What is the range of temperatures in each city?

Sections C and E

1 Here are some caterpillars, drawn full-size. Find the median length of the caterpillars in millimetres and the range of their lengths.

2 Find the median and range of each of these sets of data.

(a) 73 kg, 85 kg, 102 kg, 56 kg, 88 kg, 98 kg, 75 kg

(b) 7.6 m, 8.2 m, 6.9 m, 9 m, 6.8 m, 10.1 m, 6.8 m, 8 m

(c) 5°C, ⁻2°C, 0°C, 3°C, ⁻5°C, 1°C, 2°C

(d) 36.8°C, 37.2°C, 39.6°C, 39.2°C, 38.4°C, 37.7°C, 36.9°C

3 In Britain there are two types of squirrels, red and grey.
These are the weights of two samples of squirrels.

Red   278 g 297 g 303 g 282 g
      291 g 299 g 286 g 295 g

Grey 542 g 654 g 596 g 562 g
      636 g 602 g 582 g 613 g

How do the weights of the red and grey squirrels compare?

4 These are the 400 metre times (in seconds) for two runners. How do the two runners compare?

Jo   80.5, 79.3, 81.2, 78.3, 81.7, 80.1, 79.8

Jay   82.2, 84.3, 81.2, 80.8, 76.2, 84.5, 78.0, 82.9

5 Draw diagrams, like the one on the right to summarise the data in question 4.

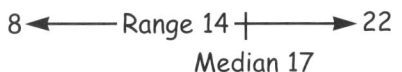

8 ◄——— Range 14 ┼———► 22
Median 17

19

Section H

1   Here are the ages of the people on a group holiday.
Find the median age.

22, 22, 22, 23, 23, 23, 23, 24, 24, 25, 25, 25, 26, 26, 26, 27, 28

2   The ages of another group are summarised in this table.

Age	21	22	23	24	25	26	27
Number of people	4	3	2	2	5	3	4

(a) How many people are there in the group?

(b) What is the median age of the group?

3   The ages of a third group are summarised in this table.

Age	21	22	23	24	25	26	27
Number of people	3	4	5	4	4	3	1

What is the median age of the group?

4   Nina did a survey of how many TVs people had at home.
Here is a summary of her data.

Number of TVs	0	1	2	3	4	5
Number of homes	3	13	9	4	3	1

What is the median number of TVs?

5   This chart shows the ages
of a group of students.

Find the median age of
the group.

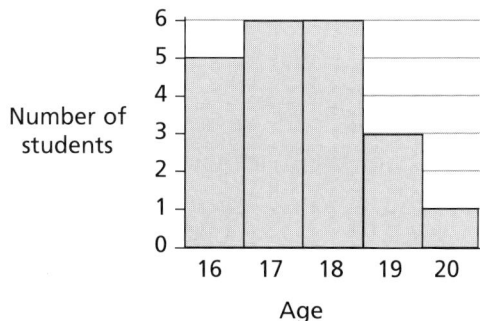

⑨ Fractions

Section A

1 Copy these and fill in the missing numbers.

    (a) $\frac{1}{4} = \frac{}{32}$ (b) $\frac{2}{3} = \frac{}{21}$ (c) $\frac{3}{5} = \frac{}{45}$

2 Simplify each of these fraction as far as possible.

    (a) $\frac{15}{35}$ (b) $\frac{25}{40}$ (c) $\frac{15}{24}$ (d) $\frac{16}{80}$ (e) $\frac{14}{42}$

3 Write each of these decimals as a fraction, as simply as possible.

    (a) 0.44   (b) 0.34   (c) 0.04   (d) 0.55   (e) 0.3

Section B

1 Which is the larger fraction in each pair?

    (a) $\frac{2}{3}, \frac{5}{8}$ (b) $\frac{3}{7}, \frac{2}{5}$ (c) $\frac{5}{6}, \frac{7}{9}$

2 Write each of these mixed numbers as an improper fraction.

    (a) $1\frac{1}{5}$ (b) $1\frac{3}{8}$ (c) $2\frac{1}{3}$ (d) $2\frac{7}{8}$ (e) $3\frac{1}{4}$

3 Write each of these improper fractions as a mixed number.

    (a) $\frac{6}{4}$ (b) $\frac{12}{5}$ (c) $\frac{15}{4}$ (d) $\frac{8}{3}$ (e) $\frac{20}{6}$

4 Work these out.

    (a) $\frac{1}{4} + \frac{1}{5}$ (b) $\frac{5}{8} + \frac{1}{3}$ (c) $\frac{2}{3} + \frac{1}{7}$ (d) $\frac{2}{5} + \frac{3}{8}$

    (e) $\frac{3}{4} + \frac{1}{3}$ (f) $\frac{4}{5} + \frac{3}{10}$ (g) $\frac{5}{6} + \frac{5}{8}$ (h) $\frac{5}{12} + \frac{2}{3}$

5 Work these out.

    (a) $\frac{3}{4} - \frac{2}{5}$ (b) $\frac{7}{8} - \frac{6}{7}$ (c) $\frac{7}{20} - \frac{1}{4}$ (d) $\frac{9}{10} - \frac{1}{4}$

    (e) $\frac{1}{2} - \frac{2}{7}$ (f) $\frac{8}{9} - \frac{1}{6}$ (g) $\frac{2}{3} - \frac{1}{9}$ (h) $1\frac{1}{2} - \frac{5}{7}$

6 Work out   (a) $4 \times \frac{7}{8}$ (b) $\frac{2}{3} \times 5$ (c) $12 \times \frac{5}{8}$

⑩ Area

Section A

1 Find the area of each of these parallelograms.

(a)

2.5 cm
6.0 cm

(b)

1.5 cm 1.0 cm
7.0 cm

(e)

2.5 cm
1.5 cm
10.5 cm

(c)

6.4 cm
3.5 cm

(d)

2 cm
0.5 cm
9.4 cm

(f)

2.5 cm 3.0 cm
7.0 cm

(h)

1.5 cm
8.4 cm 9.5 cm

(g)

3 cm 4.5 cm
8.5 cm

2 The area of each of these parallelograms is 36 cm².
Find the missing length in each one.

(a)

?
3 cm

(b)

?
8 cm

(c)

11 cm 9 cm
?

(d)

6 cm 7 cm
?

Section B

1 Put these triangles into groups so that the triangles in each group have the same area.

For each group say

- which triangles are in it
- what the areas of the triangles are

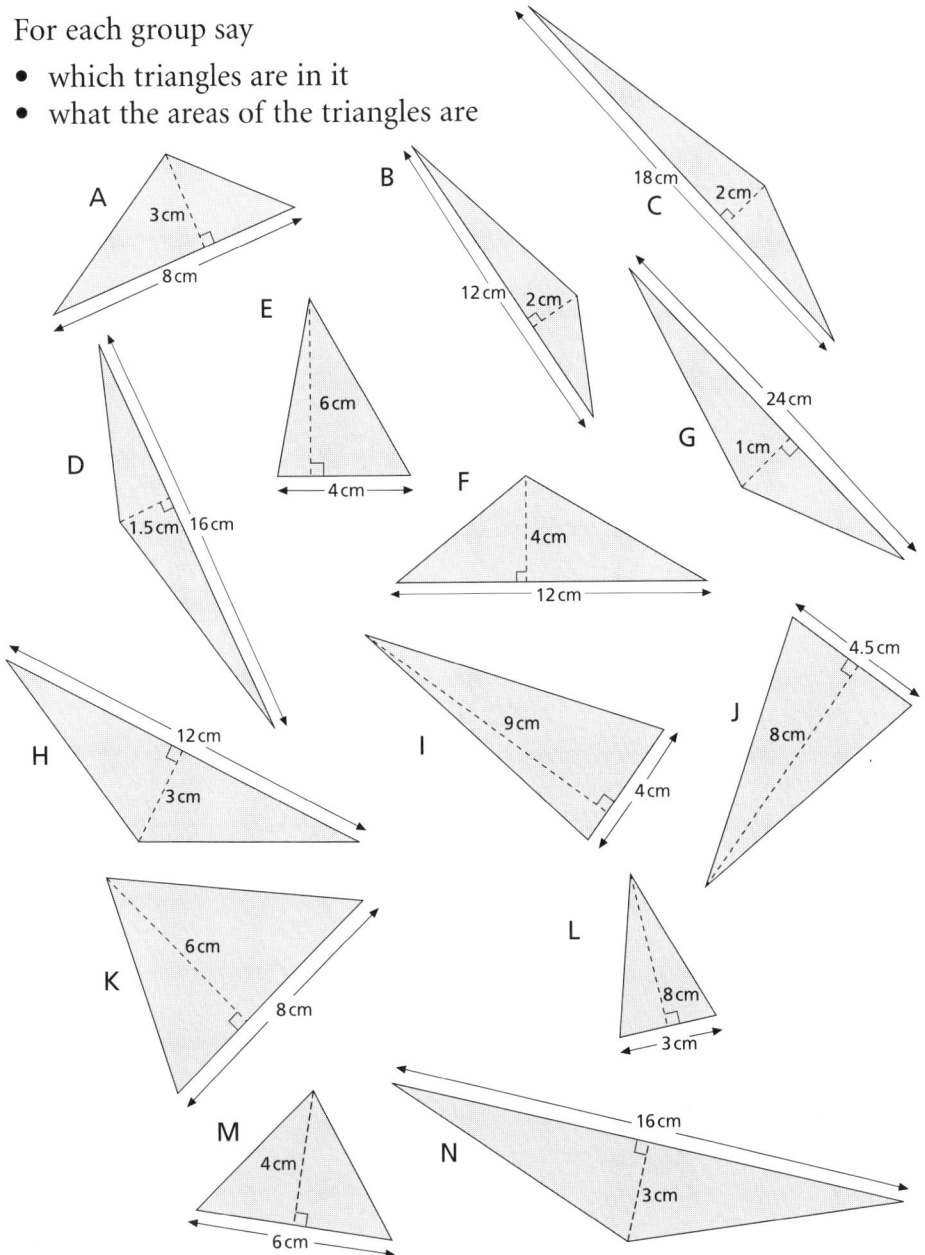

2 Find the area of each of these triangles.
They are not drawn accurately.

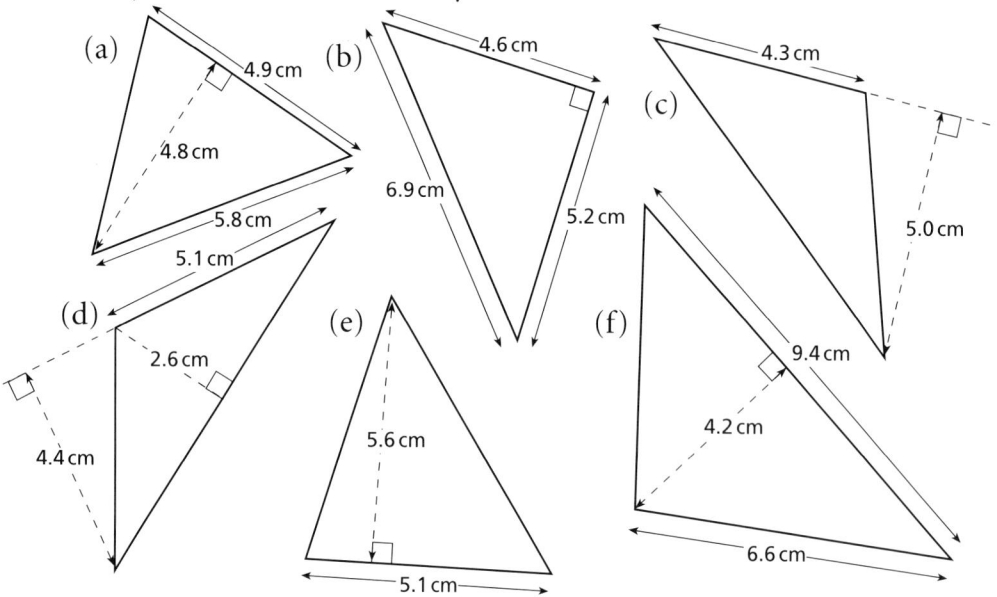

(a)

4.9 cm

4.8 cm

5.8 cm

5.1 cm

(b)

4.6 cm

6.9 cm

5.2 cm

(c)

4.3 cm

5.0 cm

(d)

2.6 cm

4.4 cm

(e)

5.6 cm

5.1 cm

(f)

9.4 cm

4.2 cm

6.6 cm

3 Work out the shaded areas by taking
appropriate measurements.

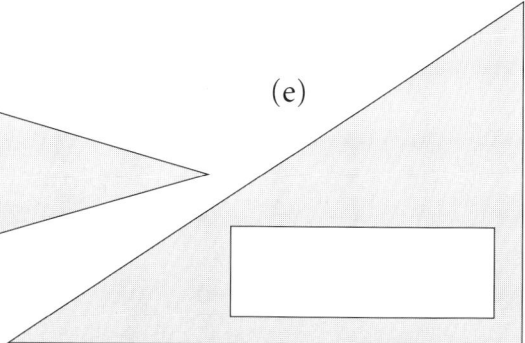

(a)

(b)

(c)

(d)

(e)

24

Section C

1 Put these trapeziums into groups so that the trapeziums in each group have the same area.

For each group say

- which trapeziums are in it
- what the area of each trapezium is

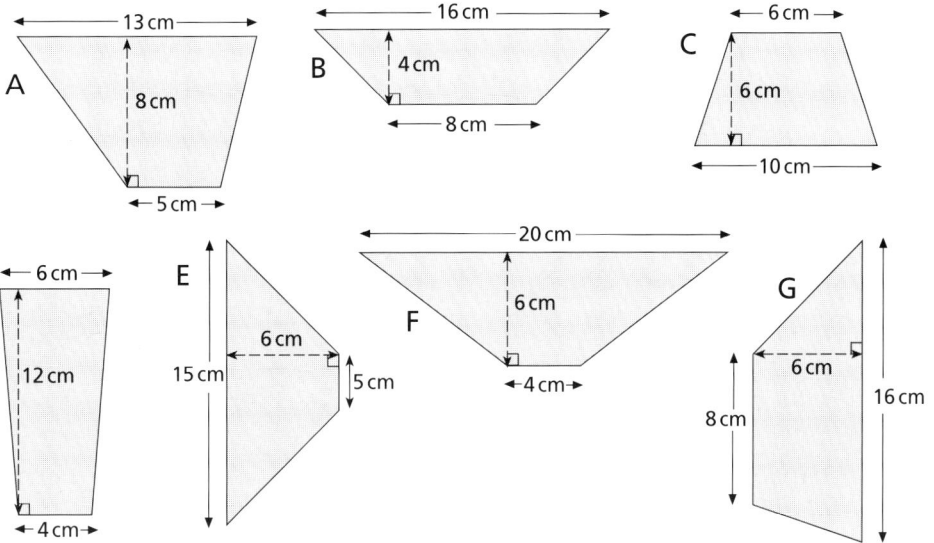

2 This diagram shows the roof of a house. It is made up of two identical triangles and two identical trapeziums.

Calculate the area of the roof.

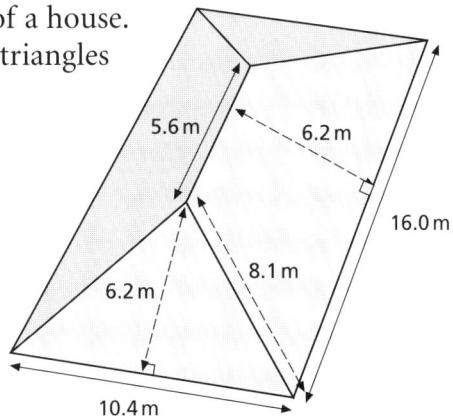

Mixed questions 1

1 Steve has these cards.

| 2 | 3 | 4 | 5 | 6 | 7 | 8 | 9 |

He shuffles them and puts them face down.

His friend Jack picks up a card. What is the probability that the number on Jack's card is

(a) greater than 3   (b) an odd number   (c) a prime number

(d) a square number   (e) a cube number   (d) greater than 9

2 (a) What is the order of rotation symmetry of each of these designs?

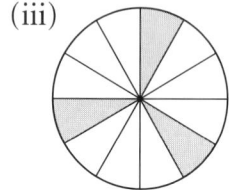

(b) Copy design (i) and shade it so that it has rotation symmetry of order 4.

(c) How many lines of reflection symmetry does each design in part (a) have?

3 Copy and complete each of these factor trees.
   (The two letter Cs both stand for the same number, and so on.)

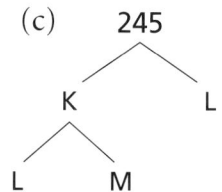

4 In this number grid, the rule across is '+ 3' and the rule down is '– 2'.

(a) Copy the grid and write expressions for the numbers in the blank squares.

(b) Find an expression for the total of all the numbers in the grid.
Write it as simply as possible.

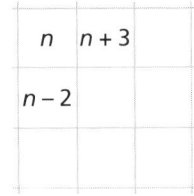

5 In this question you may use only a ruler and compasses.

(a) Draw a line and mark a point A on it.
Construct a right angle at A.

(b) Mark a point B on your first line.
Construct a square one of whose sides is AB.

(c) Draw the diagonals of the square and label their point of intersection C.

(d) Put your compasses point at A and draw an arc through C.
Mark with dots the points where the arc crosses the sides of the square.

(e) Now do the same from each other corner of the square.

(f) Join the dots with straight line segments.
What shape have you made?

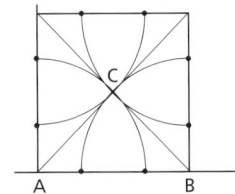

6 The number of seats sold for the 20 performances of a play were as follows:

42 45 38 38 30 27 40 31 22 18
 9 12 17 21   9 14 25 14 34 37

Find the median and range of the number of seats sold.

7 Calculate the area of this field.

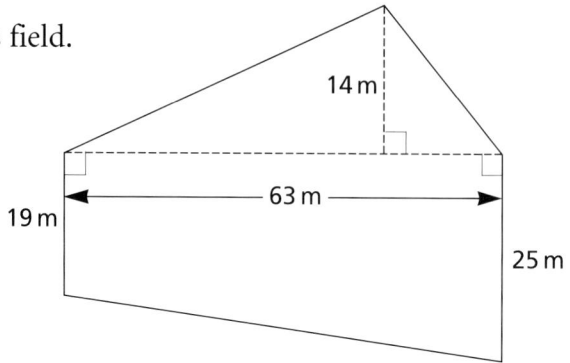

14 m

63 m

19 m

25 m

8 A farmer dies, leaving instructions in her will as to how the farmland is to be divided up between her four children.

The eldest is to get one third, the next one quarter, the next one fifth and the youngest the rest.

What fraction does the youngest get?

9 What fraction of this field is shaded?

40 m

16 m

24 m

10 Pritti has a spinner like this.
The probability that the arrow lands on grey is $\frac{1}{2}$.

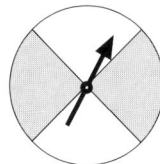

She replaces the circular base by a rectangular one.
Is the probability that the arrow lands on grey still $\frac{1}{2}$?
Explain the reason for your answer.

⑪ Inputs and outputs

Sections A and B

Copy and complete the tables.

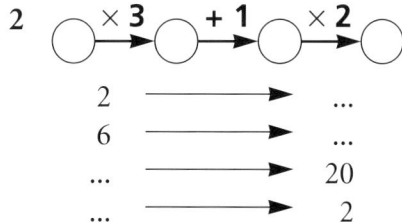

1

$$\bigcirc \xrightarrow{+\,3} \bigcirc \xrightarrow{\times\,2} \bigcirc \xrightarrow{-\,4} \bigcirc$$

1	⟶	...
4	⟶	...
...	⟶	14
...	⟶	22

2

$$\bigcirc \xrightarrow{\times\,3} \bigcirc \xrightarrow{+\,1} \bigcirc \xrightarrow{\times\,2} \bigcirc$$

2	⟶	...
6	⟶	...
...	⟶	20
...	⟶	2

3 Copy and complete these arrow diagrams.
Write each of them as shorthand rules.

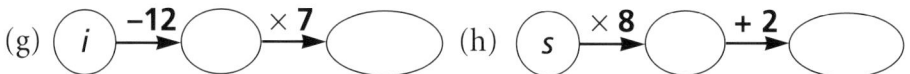

(a) $a \xrightarrow{-\,3} \bigcirc \xrightarrow{\times\,4} \bigcirc$

(b) $a \xrightarrow{\times\,4} \bigcirc \xrightarrow{-\,3} \bigcirc$

(c) $e \xrightarrow{\div\,2} \bigcirc \xrightarrow{-\,1} \bigcirc$

(d) $e \xrightarrow{-\,1} \bigcirc \xrightarrow{\div\,2} \bigcirc$

(e) $g \xrightarrow{\times\,3} \bigcirc \xrightarrow{-\,6} \bigcirc$

(f) $h \xrightarrow{+\,8} \bigcirc \xrightarrow{\div\,4} \bigcirc$

(g) $i \xrightarrow{-12} \bigcirc \xrightarrow{\times\,7} \bigcirc$

(h) $s \xrightarrow{\times\,8} \bigcirc \xrightarrow{+\,2} \bigcirc$

4 Draw arrow diagrams for these rules.

(a) $p \to 2p + 3$

(b) $m \to 2m + 6$

(c) $x \to 2(x + 3)$

(d) $b \to \frac{b}{3} + 10$

(e) $t \to \frac{t + 4}{3}$

(f) $n \to 5(n + 1)$

(g) $s \to 10(2s + 1)$

(h) $c \to 5(3 + 4c)$

Sections C and D

1 Work out the value of these.

(a) $2(x + 1)$ when   (i) $x = 4$ (ii) $x = 10$ (iii) $x = 0$

(b) $6p - 1$ when   (i) $p = 6$ (ii) $p = 0$ (iii) $p = 20$

(c) $\frac{a+3}{2}$ when   (i) $a = 1$ (ii) $a = {}^-1$ (iii) $a = 10$

2 Which of these expressions do **not** have the value 10 when $m = 3$?

$2m + 4$ $\qquad\qquad$ $3m + 1$ $\qquad\qquad$ $2(m + 2)$ $\qquad\qquad$ $3(m + 1)$

$\qquad\quad$ $4m - 2$ $\qquad\qquad$ $10(m - 2)$ $\qquad\qquad$ $5(m + 1)$

3 Work out the value of each of these when $x = 0$

(a) $4(x + 1)$ $\qquad\qquad$ (b) $4x + 1$ $\qquad\qquad$ (c) $6x - 5$

(d) $\frac{x+7}{2}$ $\qquad\qquad$ (e) $3(10 + x)$ $\qquad\qquad$ (f) $\frac{x}{2} - 4$

4 Find what you have to replace **?** by, so that whatever the input,
the two outputs are the same.

(a)

(b)

(c)

(d)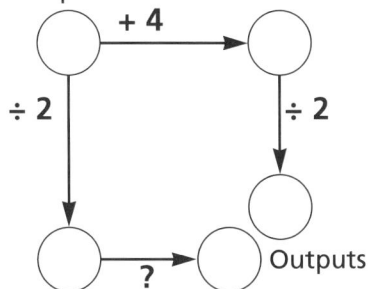

Sections E and F

1 Copy and complete these, filling in the missing numbers.

(a) $2(x + 3) = 2x + \heartsuit$

(b) $\blacktriangle(x + 4) = \blacktriangle x + 16$

(c) $5x + 10 = \bullet(x + \blacksquare)$

(d) $\dfrac{x - \blacktriangledown}{2} = \dfrac{x}{\blacklozenge} - 4$

(e) $\dfrac{x + 12}{\bullet} = \dfrac{x}{2} + \ast$

(f) $\ast(x + 6) = \ast x + 24$

2 Find an equivalent expression for each of these.

(a) $2(a + 3)$

(b) $5(x - 1)$

(c) $\dfrac{p + 8}{4}$

(d) $10(p + 4)$

(e) $4(s + 2\frac{1}{2})$

(f) $100(c - 1)$

(g) $\dfrac{y - 3}{2}$

(h) $30(m - 0.2)$

(i) $4(2a - 1)$

(j) $\dfrac{4j + 2}{2}$

(k) $\dfrac{8k - 24}{4}$

(l) $5(8a - 2)$

3 With each puzzle, describe what happens for different starting numbers and explain using algebra.

(a) Think of a number.
Add on 3.
Multiply it by 2.
Subtract 2.
Divide by 2.
Subtract your first number.
I can tell you your answer.

(b) Think of a number.
Multiply it by 5.
Add on 10.
Divide by 5.
Double it.
Subtract 4.
What is your answer?

(c) Think of a number.
Subtract 1.
Multiply by 3.
Add 6.
Divide by 3.
Subtract 1.
What is your answer?

(d) Think of a number.
Multiply by 10.
Subtract 5.
Divide by 5.
Multiply by 3.
Add 3.
What is your answer?

⑫ Decimals

Section A

Do these without a calculator.

1 (a) 0.52×0.1 (b) $0.52 \div 0.1$ (c) 6.34×0.01 (d) $6.34 \div 0.01$

2 What number is missing in each of these?
    (a) $3.47 \div \mathbf{?} = 0.0347$ (b) $3.47 \times \mathbf{?} = 0.0347$ (c) $0.682 \times \mathbf{?} = 682$
    (d) $68.2 \div \mathbf{?} = 6820$ (e) $5.03 \div \mathbf{?} = 50.3$ (f) $\mathbf{?} \times 90.4 = 0.904$

Section B

1 Work these out without a calculator.
    (a) 0.30×50 (b) 30×50 (c) 0.03×500 (d) 300×0.5

2 Work these out without a calculator.
    (a) 7×400 (b) 0.08×200 (c) 900×400
    (d) 0.1×6000 (e) 0.4×0.5 (f) 0.06×3000

3 Here is a set of numbers:

    300   30   3   0.3   0.03
       400   40   4   0.4   0.04

    From this set, find as many pairs as possible whose product is
    (a) 120   (b) 90   (c) 1.2   (d) 16   (e) 0.12

Sections C and D

1 Round these to one significant figure
    (a) 0.471   (b) 7401   (c) 21.93   (d) 54 431
    (e) 9.48   (f) 0.744   (g) 0.018 92   (h) 0.000 847

2 Estimate these by rounding the numbers to 1 s.f.
Show the numbers you use to get your estimate.
The first is done as an example.

(a) 42×79 *Estimate: 40 x 80 = 3200*

(b) 310×47 (c) 592×320 (d) 5482×376

(e) 47.2×9.8 (f) 0.3129×0.408 (g) 7.721×85.6

(h) 5725×0.82 (i) 409×0.0081 (j) 0.026×27.381

3 1 gallon is approximately equal to 4.55 litres.
A tank holds 3120 gallons of diesel.

Approximately how many litres is this?

4 About how much would 37 litres
of unleaded petrol cost?

> **PETROL**
> prices per litre
> Unleaded   82.1p
> 4 star   87.5p

Section E

Do these without a calculator.

1 (a) 23.1×0.7 (b) 0.3×0.37 (c) 450×0.4 (d) 4.56×0.005

2 You are told that $7 \times 68 = 476$.
Write down the answer to each of these.

(a) 0.7×6.8 (b) 70×0.68 (c) 0.007×6.8 (d) 0.07×6800

Sections F and G

1 Work these out.

(a) $\dfrac{2.8}{0.4}$ (b) $\dfrac{0.72}{0.09}$ (c) $\dfrac{3.6}{0.04}$ (d) $\dfrac{60}{0.02}$ (e) $\dfrac{270}{0.9}$

2 Work these out.

(a) $\dfrac{1.44}{0.6}$ (b) $\dfrac{384}{0.08}$ (c) $\dfrac{10.36}{700}$ (d) $\dfrac{51.2}{40}$ (e) $\dfrac{150}{0.06}$

Section H

1 Round each of these numbers to 2 s.f.
    (a) 48 120   (b) 0.042 124   (c) 9.082   (d) 0.003 713

2 Round each of these numbers to 3 s.f.
    (a) 871.36   (b) 0.041 856   (c) 27.835   (d) 310.275

3 (a) Round 0.004 8146 to 3 s.f.   (b) Round 9.008 315 to 2 s.f.
    (c) Round 4 305 609 to 4 s.f.   (d) Round 420.573 to 3 s.f.

Section I

1 (a) Round 67 810 to the nearest hundred. (b) Round 67 810 to 2 s.f.
    (c) Round 5.4367 to one decimal place. (d) Round 5.4367 to 1 s.f.

2 (a) Round 0.040 32 to 2 d.p.   (b) Round 0.040 32 to 2 s.f.
    (c) Round 8712.48 to the nearest ten.   (d) Round 8712.48 to 1 d.p.

*3 The number in this headline has been rounded to the nearest hundred.

> **Singer attracts 6700 fans**
> Star performer Bianca Rossa delighted the hundreds of fans who flocked to hear

    (a) Which of these could have been the actual number of fans?
          6500   6683   6772   6641   6731   6702
    (b) What is the smallest actual number that would fit the headline?
    (c) What is the largest number that would fit the headline?

*4 The number in this headline has been rounded to the nearest thousand.

> **Student earns £28 000 in summer holidays**
> Computer science student Nadia Picozzi worked for local firm Update during her

    (a) Which of these could have been the actual amount Nadia earned?
         £29 000   £27 800   £26 950   £28 640   £28 428   £27 462
    (b) What is the smallest actual amount that would fit the headline?
    (c) What is the largest amount that would fit the headline?

⑭ Parallel lines

Section A

1 (a) Draw two parallel lines 4 cm apart.

   (b) Draw another pair 4 cm apart,
       crossing the first pair.

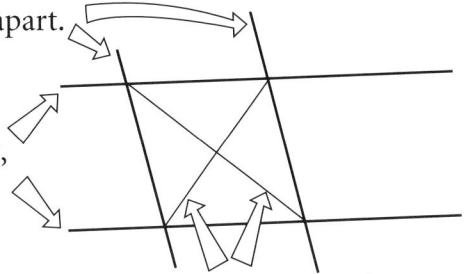

   (c) Draw these diagonals.
       Measure angles and lengths
       and write what you find.

2 Jack is at point J on an
   orienteering challenge.

   He runs parallel to
   the wall ZY until he
   reaches the river XY.

   What are the
   coordinates of the
   point he reaches?

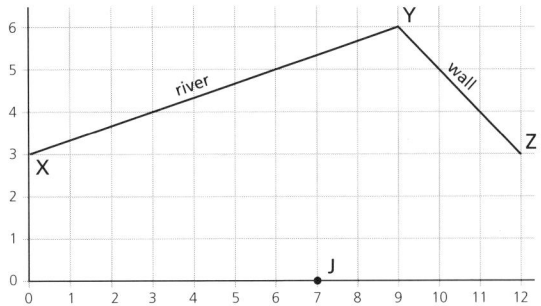

3 P, Q and R are buoys marking the site of a ship wreck.
   Harry is searching for sunken treasure.
   He has been given these directions:

   Draw a line joining P to Q.
   Draw a line joining Q to R.
   Draw a line through A parallel to PQ.
   Draw a line through B parallel to QR.
   The cargo hold is directly below
   where these two lines meet.

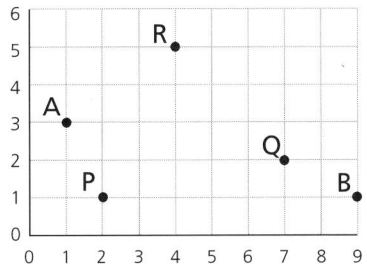

   Copy the diagram on to squared paper.
   Use the directions to find the coordinates of the cargo hold.

Sections C and D

1
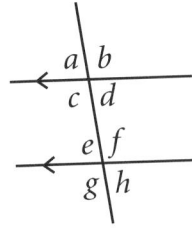

| corresponding angles |
| alternate angles |
| vertically opposite angles |
| supplementary angles |

Copy and complete each sentence with the correct phrase.

Angles a and d are ....   Angles e and a are ....

Angles c and f are ....   Angles f and d are ....

Angles h and d are ....   Angles f and e are ....

Angles f and g are ....   Angles b and f are ....

2   Work out the angles marked with letters.
    Explain your results.

(a)

(b)

(c)

(d)
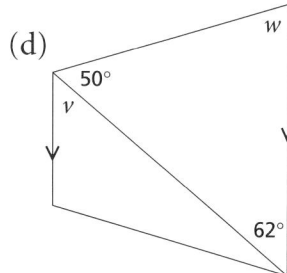

3   Work out the angles marked with letters.

(a)

(b)
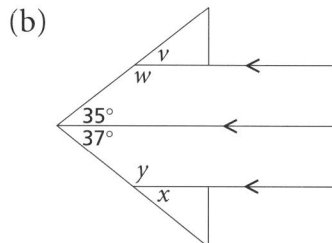

4 Work out the angles marked with a letter.
If you need to, copy the sketch and add extra lines and angles.

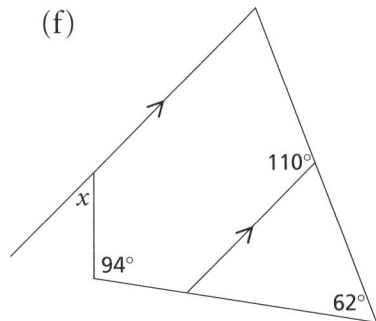

(a)

p

$72°$

$63°$

q

(b)

$48°$

$110°$

r

s

(c)

$88°$

$30°$

u

t

$120°$

(d)

v

$115°$

$52°$

(e)

$98°$

w

$130°$

$110°$

(f)

$110°$

x

$94°$

$62°$

5 Work out each angle marked with a **?**.
Give reasons.

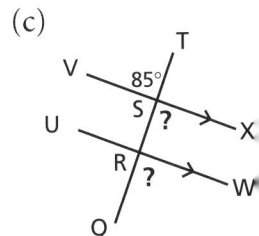

(a)

A B
E F
D ?
C 80°
G H

(b)

I J
K L ? ? N
110° M
O P

(c)

V T
85°
U S ?
R X
? W
Q

37

⑮ Percentage

Section A

1 This diagram shows the proportions of protein, fat and carbohydrate
   in two chocolate bars.

Cadbury's Double Decker

0%   100%

Sainsbury's Creamy White

protein   carbohydrate   fat

   What are the percentages of protein, fat and carbohydrate in each bar?

2 These diagrams show the proportions of protein, carbohydrate, fat
   and fibre in two cereals.

protein

carbohydrate

fat

fibre

Quaker Oats   All Bran

   Which of the percentages on the right is nearest to
   (a) the percentage of fibre in All Bran
   (b) the percentage of protein in Quaker Oats
   (c) the percentage of carbohydrate in Quaker Oats
   (d) the percentage of carbohydrate in All Bran?

10%
30%
50%
70%
90%

Section B

No calculator!

1   Work out these in your head.
    (a) 50% of £20   (b) 50% of £17   (c) 50% of £90

2   Work out these in your head.
    (a) 25% of £60   (b) 25% of £52   (c) 25% of £50

3   Work out these in your head.
    (a) 10% of 70 kg   (b) 10% of £75   (c) 10% of £73

4   Do these in your head. Just write the answer.
    (a) 1% of £5   (b) 3% of £5   (c) 97% of £5
    (d) 1% of £90   (e) 5% of £90

5   (a) How do you work out 10% of a number in your head?
    (b) How do you work out 5% of a number in your head?
    (c) How do you work out 15% of a number in your head?

6   In your head, work these out.
    (a) 15% of £10   (b) 15% of £40   (c) 15% of £90

7   Find the odd one out in each block.

(a)
| 50% of £6 |
| 3% of £10 |
| 25% of £12 |
| 10% of £30 |

(b)
| 10% of £50 |
| 100% of £5 |
| 5% of £100 |
| 25% of £20 |
| 75% of £8 |

(c)
| 25% of £18 |
| 10% of £45 |
| 5% of £80 |
| 9% of £50 |

Section C

1   What decimal is equivalent to
    (a) 68%   (b) 41%   (c) 80%   (d) 8%
    (e) 9%   (f) 90%   (g) 54.5%   (h) 30.5%

2   What percentage is equivalent to
    (a) 0.65   (b) 0.6   (c) 0.06   (d) 0.065
    (e) 0.02   (f) 0.22   (g) 0.2   (h) 0.202

3   Copy and complete
    this table.

Fraction		Decimal		Percentage
$\frac{58}{100}$	=		=	
	=	0.32	=	
$\frac{9}{100}$	=		=	
	=		=	80%
	=	0.05	=	

4   Put these in order, starting with the smallest.
    (a) $\frac{8}{100}$ $\frac{81}{100}$ 0.09 7% 0.8 0.1
    (b) 20% $\frac{1}{2}$ 0.02 0.1 12% 0.7
    (c) 75% $\frac{8}{100}$ $\frac{3}{10}$ 0.07 40% 0.3

Section D

1   Match an answer with each
    calculation, and write an
    answer for the extra calculation.

Calculation	Answer
28% of 4	0.64
47% of 220	6.643
91% of 7.3	1.12
26% of 82	103.4
8% of 8	

2   Find the odd one out.
    A   20% of £50   B   30% of £20   C   75% of £8

3   Find the odd one out.
    A   64% of 5 kg   B   44% of 7.5 kg   C   60% of 5.5 kg

4   A car is normally priced at £7995. In a sale, 15% is taken off the price.
    (a) How much is taken off?
    (b) How much does the car cost in the sale?

5 The Southern Stone Building Society pays 5% interest per year on accounts that have less than £10 000, and 6% on other accounts. How much interest will the following earn in a year?

(a) Winston, who has £8210   (b) Julie, who has £605 100

(c) Hadley, who has £47 600

Sections E and F

1 Put these fractions in order of size, smallest first. $\frac{6}{11}$ $\frac{11}{19}$ $\frac{13}{27}$

2 13 out of 17 apples are rotten.
What percentage (to the nearest 1%) are rotten?

3 In a school of 672 pupils, 83 are absent during a flu epidemic.
What percentage (to the nearest 1%) is absent?

4 A piece of fruit weighed 67.8 g when it was picked.
After heating to remove water it weighed 21.1 g.

(a) What percentage of the fruit was left after heating?

(b) What percentage of the unheated fruit was water?

5 Find the odd one out by changing each to a percentage.

A 42 out of 168   **B** 35.5 out of 144   **C** 67.25 out of 269

6 Find the odd one out.

A 2.22 out of 3.7   **B** 2.24 out of 4   **C** 2.16 out of 3.6

7 In 1994 the population of the UK was 58.4 million.
48.7 million lived in England, 5.1 million in Scotland,
2.9 million in Wales and the rest in Northern Ireland.

(a) What percentage of the UK population lived in Scotland?

(b) What percentage lived in England and Wales together?

(c) What percentage lived in Northern Ireland?

Sections G and H

1 Here is the breakdown of samples of two breakfast cereals.

	Protein	Carbohydrate	Fat	Fibre
Quaker Oats	11.0 g	62.0 g	8.0 g	7.0 g
All Bran	13 g	46 g	3.5 g	29 g

(a) Draw a pie chart to illustrate the data for Quaker Oats.

(b) Draw a pie chart to illustrate the data for All Bran.

(c) How do the charts compare?
Write about any similarities or differences.

2 Here is a table of the energy consumed in the UK
(in equivalent million tonnes of oil).

	Coal	Petroleum	Natural gas	Nuclear
1982	68.0	71.0	45.2	11.9
1995	49.8	76.2	70.0	21.4

(a) Draw two pie charts to illustrate the data.

(b) How do the charts compare?
Write about any similarities or differences.

3 Peter bought some postcards at a stamp and postcard fair.
The seller rounded down the price from £2.30 to £2.

(a) How much discount did he get?

(b) Calculate what percentage the discount is of £2.30.

4 Copy and complete these tables.

(a)

of	5	82	
10%	0.5		
20%			10
	3.5		

(b)

of	30	55	
30%			6
80%			
		11	

16 Think of a number

Section A

1 Solve these puzzles by using arrow diagrams.

(a)
> I think of a number.
> - I subtract 7.
> - I multiply by 7.4.
>
> The result is 185.
> What number did I think of?

(b)
> I think of a number.
> - I multiply by 0.5.
> - I add 1.5.
>
> The result is 6.
> What number did I think of?

(c)
> I think of a number.
> - I add 5.
> - I divide by 0.3.
> - I subtract 17.
>
> The result is 9.
> What number did I think of?

(d)
> I think of a number.
> - I divide by 6.
> - I subtract 1.4.
> - I multiply by 0.2.
>
> The result is 8.
> What number did I think of?

2 The result for this number puzzle is missing.

(a) Choose a number for the result.
   Solve the number puzzle for your result.

(b) Solve the number puzzle for some
   different results.

(c) What do you notice?
   Try to explain this.

> I think of a number.
> - I add 1.
> - I multiply by 4.
> - I add 6.
> - I divide by 2.
> - I subtract 5.
>
> The result is
> What num

Section B

1 Write an equation for this
number puzzle.
Use *n* to stand for the number.

> I think of a number.
> - I multiply by 54.
>
> The result is 378.
> What number did I think of?

2 Write an equation for each of these number puzzles.
Use n to stand for the number each time.

(a)
> *I think of a number.*
> - *I multiply by 7.*
> - *I add 3.*
>
> *The result is 206.*
> *What number did I think of?*

(b)
> *I think of a number.*
> - *I subtract 13.*
> - *I divide by 4.*
>
> *The result is 6.1.*
> *What number did I think of?*

3 Write an equation for each arrow diagram.

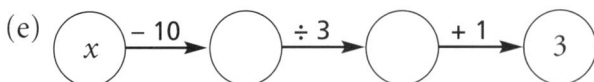

(a) y → -3 → ○ → $\times 7$ → 21

(b) a → $\div 5$ → ○ → $+3$ → 18

(c) p → $\times 3.2$ → ○ → $\div 7$ → 4

(d) m → $+9$ → ○ → $\times 5.1$ → 102

(e) x → -10 → ○ → $\div 3$ → ○ → $+1$ → 3

Section C

1 Solve these equations by using arrow diagrams.

(a) $11(w + 7) = 198$
(b) $7n - 5 = 51$
(c) $12p + 3 = 375$

(d) $\frac{x}{3} - 2 = 3.1$
(e) $\frac{a + 3}{4} = 20$
(f) $\frac{y - 3}{8} = 4.5$

(g) $17(p - 5) = 306$
(h) $\frac{h}{6} + 5 = 7.7$
(i) $\frac{t + 4}{13} = 12$

2 Solve these equations.

(a) $7x - 4.7 = 31$
(b) $6a + 3.2 = 29$
(c) $0.2y - 4 = 6$

(d) $\frac{m}{7} + 4.4 = 5$
(e) $\frac{w - 4.9}{5.2} = 2$
(f) $0.4(h - 2) = 3.8$

(g) $32(k + 1.5) = 480$
(h) $\frac{m + 8.1}{2.5} = 90$
(i) $\frac{n}{2.9} - 11 = 5$

3 Make up three different equations that have $x = 4$ as a solution.

4 Make up two different equations that have $p = 2.5$ as a solution.

5 Make up two different equations that have $n = 7.1$ as a solution.

6 Solve these equations.

(a) $5(x - 7) - 13 = 32$

(b) $2.5(d + 16) - 69 = 6$

(c) $\dfrac{y - 6}{3.4} + 1.5 = 5$

(d) $\dfrac{6m}{2.1} - 4 = 16$

(e) $\dfrac{b + 4.3}{0.6} - 29 = 6$

(f) $\dfrac{7n - 16}{4} + 34 = 58$

*7 The numbers p, q, r and s are connected by the formula
$$s = pq + r$$
Work out

(a) the value of s when $p = 4.5$, $q = 1.2$ and $r = 7.5$

(b) the value of r when $s = 10.5$, $p = 1.5$ and $q = 6$

(c) the value of q when $s = 16.5$, $p = 3.5$ and $r = 8.1$

(d) the value of p when $s = 8$, $q = 0.4$ and $r = 4.6$

*8 The numbers w, x, y and z are connected by the formula
$$w = \frac{x}{y} - z$$
Work out the value of x when $w = 1.4$, $y = 5$ and $z = 0.2$.

⑰ Quadrilaterals

Section B

1 For this question, work on square dotty paper if you like.
Do drawings to show how

(a) a square can be split into two trapeziums

(b) a rhombus can be split into two parallelograms

(c) a kite can be split into a rhombus and an arrowhead

(d) a rectangle can be split into two trapeziums and a parallelogram

(e) a square can be split into two arrowheads and a rhombus

Section C

1 Work out the angles marked with letters.

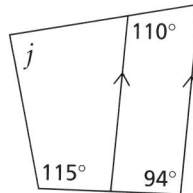

2 Work out the angles marked with letters.

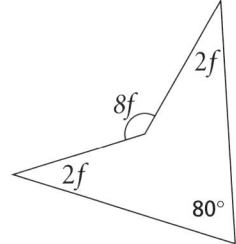

Section D

1 Do accurate drawings of the quadrilaterals sketched here.

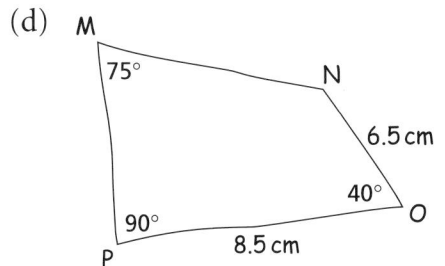

(a)

(b)

(c)

(d)

⑱ Negative numbers

Sections A and B

1 Work these out.

(a) $^-9 + {}^-4$ (b) $^-8 - {}^-2$ (c) $3 - {}^-6$ (d) $^-2 - {}^-7$

2 Given that $x = {}^-3$ and $y = {}^-5$, find the value of

(a) $2x + 1$ (b) $10 - y$ (c) $4 - 3x$ (d) $4y + 5$ (e) $2x - 3y$

3 Given that $a = 4$ and $b = {}^-8$, find the value of

(a) $^-12 - 3a$ (b) $3 - 7a$ (c) $11 - 2b$ (d) $3b + 5$ (e) $5a - 3b$

4 I think of a number, square it and subtract 7. The result is 2.
What could my number be?

5 I think of a number, square it and multiply by 4. The result is 100.
What could my number be?

Sections C and D

1 Given that $r = {}^-4$ and $s = {}^-8$, find the value of

(a) $\frac{r}{2} + 1$ (b) $5 - \frac{r}{2}$ (c) $^-2 + \frac{s}{4}$ (d) $10 - \frac{s}{2}$ (e) $\frac{s}{2} + \frac{r}{4}$

2 Given that $p = {}^-2$ and $q = {}^-3$, find the value of

(a) $\frac{10}{p} - 1$ (b) $6 + \frac{12}{q}$ (c) $13 - \frac{8}{p}$ (d) $7 - \frac{21}{q}$ (e) $\frac{6}{p} - \frac{6}{q}$

3 What is the input of this arrow diagram if the output is

(a) 1   (b) 21   (c) $^-19$

Input $\times\ ^-5$ $- 4$ Output

4 Solve these 'think of a number' problems.

(a) I think of a number, divide it by $^-3$ and subtract 6.
The result is $^-8$.

(b) I think of a number, subtract 4 and multiply by $^-4$.
The result is 12.

⑲ Fair to all?

Section A

1   Kathy has 6 goes at skittles. Her scores are 4, 3, 0, 6, 2, 6.
    Then Mark has 10 goes. His scores are 3, 1, 7, 5, 2, 4, 2, 7, 1, 2.

    (a) Who did better, Kathy or Mark?
        Give a reason for your answer.

    (b) If Mark had stopped after 4 goes, who would have done better?
        Give a reason.

2   The pupils in a class get these amounts of pocket money each week.

Girls	£3.90 £4.80 £4.00 £3.90 £3.40
	£3.70 £4.60 £4.00 £4.00 £3.70
Boys	£3.50 £3.50 £5.20 £3.70 £4.00
	£4.00 £4.00 £3.70

    (a) What is the mean amount of pocket money for the girls?

    (b) What is the mean amount for the boys?

3   What is the mean number of letters in the words in this question?

4   What is the mean value of the different types of ordinary
    British coins?

5   (a) Find three odd numbers that have a mean of 7.

    (b) Why is it not possible to find three even numbers that
        have a mean of 7?

6   Find five numbers that have a mean of 9.4 .

Section B

1 Three people in a family each have 28 teeth.
   The other person in the family has 26 teeth.
   What is the mean number of teeth per person in the family?

2 Steve records how many people there are in cars passing his school.

Number of occupants	Number of cars
1	50
2	25
3	20
4	3
5	2

   What is the mean number of people in a car?

3 A zoo has a family of smooth snakes, which are very rare in Britain.
   Since 1975, every time a female snake has laid eggs,
   the zoo has recorded the number of eggs.

Number of eggs	Frequency
4	5
5	1
6	4
7	1
8	9
9	5
10	10
11	2
12	8
13	1
14	4

What is the mean number of eggs laid?

4 These are the recorded weights in grams of 25 frogs that a naturalist has caught.

190 150 280 150 130 150 300 210 150 320
170 170 160 260 180 290 290 240 270 140
140 310 320 200 200

(a) Calculate the mean weight of the frogs.

(b) Draw a scale like this on graph paper.
Mark dots for all the frogs.

Weight in grams

The naturalist knows that the frogs are a mixture of marsh frogs and edible frogs. The two kinds look similar, but marsh frogs are heavier than edible frogs.

(c) From your dot plot, how many do you think are marsh frogs?

(d) Work out the mean weight of those you think are marsh frogs.

(e) Work out the mean weight of those you think are edible frogs.

Section E

1 In class of 30 pupils the mean weight of the 10 boys is 47.2 kg and the mean weight of the 20 girls is 42.4 kg.

What is the mean weight of a pupil in the class?

2 The heights of the members of a male rowing crew are

1.74 m 1.89 m 1.88 m 2.07 m 2.04 m 1.91 m 1.98 m 1.92 m

(a) Calculate their mean height.

(b) The height of the cox is 1.46 m.
Without calculating, make an estimate of the mean height of the crew if he is included in it.

(c) Now calculate the mean height with him included.

3 These are St Mary's netball results for the first 10 games of the season.

St Mary's	7	6	1	3	9	11	5	8	2	14
Opposing team	2	7	2	5	10	5	13	10	3	4

(a) What is the mean score for St Mary's?

(b) What is the mean score for the opposing teams?

(c) Did St Mary's win most of the games?
Do the answers to (a) and (b) allow you to predict this?

(d) The first game was won by a margin of 5 goals.
The second was won by a margin of 1 goal.
Work out the mean goal margin for all these games.
Do the answers to (a) and (b) allow you to predict this?

4 In a committee of six people, one member leaves and
is replaced by a new member.
As a result the mean age of the committee goes down from 42 to 39.

What does this tell you about the ages of the member who left and
the one who joined?

*5 Find a set of seven different positive whole numbers whose mean is 8,
median is 5 and range is 13.

How many different sets can you find?

Mixed questions 2

1 Copy and complete each of these.

   (a) $3(p + 5) = \ldots p + \ldots$ (b) $4q - 12 = \ldots(q - \ldots)$

   (c) $\dfrac{20r - 8}{4} = \ldots r - \ldots$ (d) $\dfrac{s + 14}{2} = \ldots s + \ldots$

2 You are told that $245 \times 106 = 25\,970$.
   Without using a calculator, write down the answer to each of these.

   (a) $2597 \div 10.6$ (b) 24.5×0.106 (c) 0.245×0.106

   (d) $2.597 \div 0.245$ (e) $259.7 \div 1060$ (f) $2597 \div 24\,500$

3 Calculate the angle marked x.
   Give a reason for each step of your working.

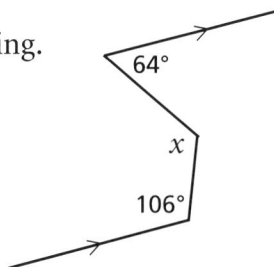

4 Without using a calculator, work these out.

   (a) 25% of £13   (b) 20% of £48   (c) 15% of £70

   (d) 30% of £28   (e) 95% of £18   (f) 12.5% of £40

5 Which of the types of quadrilateral listed below

   (a) may have just one line of reflection symmetry

   (b) cannot have just one line of reflection symmetry

   Draw diagrams, where appropriate, to illustrate your answers.

     trapezium   rhombus   parallelogram

        rectangle   kite   square

6 (a) I think of a number, multiply it by ⁻2, subtract ⁻6 and divide by ⁻3. The result is ⁻8.

What number did I think of?

(b) I think of a number, add ⁻10, multiply by 4, subtract ⁻8 and divide by ⁻4. The result is ⁻4.

What number did I think of?

7 In a football team, the mean weight of the five heaviest players is 85.2 kg. The mean weight of the six remaining players is 74.6 kg.

Calculate the mean weight of the team, to the nearest 0.1 kg.

8 The line AE shows a path across a field ABCD.
The path splits the field into two parts of equal area.
Calculate the distance BE.

9 Solve each of these equations.

(a) $3(x - 7) = 51$

(b) $\dfrac{4x + 5}{9} = 3$

(c) $\dfrac{x}{2} - 23 = 41$

(d) $3x - 17 = {}^-2$

(e) $5x + 18 = 3$

(f) $\dfrac{4x - 13}{5} = {}^-9$

10 In a club, one member aged 34 leaves and is replaced by a new member aged 64.
As a result, the mean age of the club goes up by 2 years.

How many members are there in the club?

⑳ Know your calculator

Section A

1 Work these out without a calculator.

(a) $5 + 14 \div 2$ (b) $7 \times 8 - 6$ (c) $15 + 4 \times 3$

(d) $20 - 6 \times 3$ (e) $30 \div 3 + 2$ (f) $15 + 12 \div 4$

(g) $9 \times 4 \div 3$ (h) $17 - 2 \times 3$ (i) $23 + 18 \div 3$

2 Find the missing number in each of these calculations.

(a) $17 + 12 \div \blacksquare = 20$ (b) $8 + 3 \times \blacksquare = 17$ (c) $5 + 2 \times \blacksquare = 17$

(d) $12 \div \blacksquare + 1 = 3$ (e) $14 + \blacksquare \div 3 = 18$ (f) $21 + \blacksquare \times 3 = 36$

(g) $\blacksquare + 15 \div 3 = 12$ (h) $\blacksquare \div 3 - 2 = 9$ (i) $\blacksquare \times 9 - 4 = 23$

3 You can replace each diamond in the expression below with $+, -, \times$ or $\div$.

You cannot change the order of numbers, or use brackets.

$$\boxed{36 \; \blacklozenge \; 9 \; \blacklozenge \; 3}$$

Replace each diamond with a symbol to make an expression with the value

(a) 12 (b) 33 (c) 9 (d) 108

4 In a game there are three number cards … $\boxed{4}$ $\boxed{8}$ $\boxed{16}$

… and four operation cards $\boxed{+}$ $\boxed{-}$ $\boxed{\times}$ $\boxed{\div}$.

Each time you must use all the number cards and only two operation cards, for example $\boxed{16}$ $\boxed{\times}$ $\boxed{4}$ $\boxed{-}$ $\boxed{8}$

Show how you could use the cards to make expressions with values.

(a) 18 (b) 48 (c) 12 (d) 2

Sections B and C

1 Write these expressions, adding brackets where necessary, to make the result 36 each time.

(a) $3 \times 3 \times 4$ (b) $4 \times 5 + 4$ (c) $4 + 4 \times 8$

(d) $20 - 2 \times 2$ (e) $24 + 3 \times 4$ (f) $4 \times 12 - 3$

2 Put these expressions into groups so that those in each group have the same value.

A $9 + 3 \times 4$ **B** $8 \times 3 \div 2$ **C** $20 - 3 \times 5$ **D** $36 \div (14 \div 7)$

E $15 + 18 \div 6$ **F** $30 - 3 \times 3$ **G** $35 \div (8 - 1)$ **H** $48 \div (6 - 2)$

3 Which of these expressions do not need brackets?

A $12 + (4 - 2)$ **B** $12 + (4 \times 2)$ **C** $12 \div (4 + 2)$

D $12 + (4 \div 2)$ **E** $(12 \times 4) + 2$ **F** $12 - (4 - 2)$

4 Find four matching pairs of expressions.

A $24 - \dfrac{6}{3}$ **B** $(24 - 6) \div 3$ **C** $\dfrac{24}{6} - 3$ **D** $\dfrac{24}{6 - 3}$

E $24 \div 6 - 3$ **F** $24 \div (6 - 3)$ **G** $24 - (6 \div 3)$ **H** $\dfrac{24 - 6}{3}$

5 Work these out without a calculator.

(a) $\dfrac{20}{3 + 2}$ (b) $8 + \dfrac{12}{3}$ (c) $\dfrac{18 - 3}{2}$

(d) $\dfrac{30}{5} - 5$ (e) $\dfrac{48}{3 \times 4}$ (f) $12 - \dfrac{21}{3}$

(g) $20 - 2 \times 4$ (h) $\dfrac{36}{7 - 3} - 5$

Section D

1 Find the value of each of these.

(a) $\dfrac{24.7}{6.2 - 2.4}$ (b) $31.8 - \dfrac{19.5}{2.6}$ (c) $\dfrac{4 \times 10.2}{8 \times 0.6}$

2 Find the value of each of these.

(a) $\dfrac{15 - 7.8}{1.09 + 0.35}$ (b) $\dfrac{2.4 \times 5.2}{5 - 1.8}$ (c) $(7.5 + 3.7) \times 1.2$

(d) $5 \times \dfrac{28.8}{4.5} - 2.4$ (e) $\dfrac{(8.7 - 2.3) \times 1.5}{5.1 - 4.8}$ (f) $\dfrac{3.8 \times 8.4}{12 \times 0.4}$

Section E

1 Without using a calculator, evaluate these.

(a) $30 - 5^2$ (b) 4×3^2 (c) $12 + 3 \times 3^2$ (d) $3 \times 4^2 - 8$

(e) $(5 \times 2)^2 - 6$ (f) $\dfrac{4^2}{2}$ (g) $\dfrac{36}{3^2}$ (h) $\dfrac{6^2}{2^2}$

2 Using only the keys $\boxed{(}\ \boxed{)}\ \boxed{9}\ \boxed{4}\ \boxed{+}\ \boxed{-}\ \boxed{\div}\ \boxed{\times}\ \boxed{x^2}$
write down a set of key presses to evaluate these.

(a) 9×4^2 (b) $\dfrac{9 - 4^2}{4}$ (c) $\dfrac{4 + 9^2}{4^2}$ (d) $\dfrac{9}{9 - 4^2}$

3 Evaluate these.

(a) 0.3×6^2 (b) $(2.3 + 4.2)^2$ (c) $\dfrac{6.3 - 0.5^2}{1.21}$

(d) $\dfrac{3.5 \times 4^2}{32}$ (e) $\dfrac{(2.5 \times 4.2)^2}{30 - 4.8}$ (f) $10 - \dfrac{2.4^2}{4}$

(g) $\dfrac{7.2 + 2.1^2}{0.5 \times 3.87}$ (h) $\dfrac{(10 - 2.8^2) \times 4}{1.92}$ (i) $\dfrac{2.5 + 4.7 \times 4^2}{7^2 + 6.5}$

(j) $3 \times (2.5^2 + 1.5^2)$ (k) $\dfrac{8^2 - 5^2}{8 - 5}$ (l) $\dfrac{5.6^2 - 3.2^2}{5.6 - 3.2}$

*4 Can you spot a quick way to get the answer in 3 (k) and (l) above?
Try with some other numbers. Does it always work?

Sections F and G

1 Evaluate each of these expressions.

(a) $\sqrt{22.09} - 19.2$

(b) $\sqrt{(22.09 - 19.2)}$

(c) $\sqrt{29.16 \times 9.61}$

(d) $\dfrac{37.52 + 17.77}{\sqrt{28.09} + 4.4}$

(e) $24.7 + \dfrac{11.2}{\sqrt{7.84}}$

(f) $\dfrac{\sqrt{10.24} + 6.57}{1.52 - 0.88}$

2 Evaluate these.

(a) $3.1 - 2.4 \times {}^-1.2$

(b) $10.8 \times (3.7 - 8)$

(c) $21^2 - (4 \times {}^-5)$

(d) $({}^-4 \times 7)^2 - 81$

(e) $(3 + {}^-5.5) \times (13 - {}^-2.7)$

(f) $\dfrac{{}^-12}{2.4} - 2.7$

(g) $\dfrac{({}^-6 + 3.5)^2}{1.25}$

(h) $\dfrac{{}^-18 + 21^2}{(7 - {}^-3)^2 - 6}$

(i) $\dfrac{{}^-4.2 - 6}{{}^-5 + 3.3}$

(j) $\left(\dfrac{{}^-47}{5}\right)^2 - 10.3$

(k) $\dfrac{4.6^2 - 1}{1.6^2 - 0.16}$

*3 Copy and complete this cross-number puzzle. Write decimal points on the lines between squares.

$a = 5.6$ $b = {}^-10.5$ $c = {}^-6.3$
$d = {}^-0.64$ $e = 4.8$ $f = 2.142$
$g = 62.8$

Across

1    $a + bc$

5    $\dfrac{ac}{b}$

6    $b + c^2$

8   bc

10    $c - \dfrac{a}{d}$

11    $e - ad$

Down

2    $\sqrt{(a^2 + b^2)}$

3    $a + \dfrac{f}{b}$

4    $\dfrac{b + c}{d}$

6    $a + de$

7    $2c^2 - g$

9    $\sqrt{(b^2 - c^2)} + \frac{1}{2}e$

㉑ Three dimensions

Section B

1   This shape is made with six cubes.

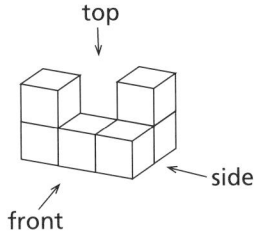

   This is the front view.
   (a) Draw a side view
   (b) Draw a top view

2   This object is made from children's building blocks.
   Draw three views of the object.

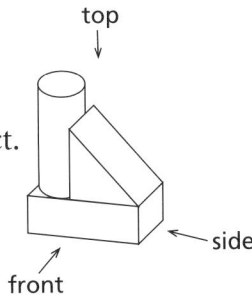

3   Draw a view of this object looking in the direction of each of the arrows A, B and C.

Section C

1   Calculate the volume of each of these cuboids.
   (a) 6.5 cm by 8 cm by 4 cm
   (b) 7.5 cm by 9 cm by 10 cm
   (c) 16 cm by 12.5 cm by 8.5 cm
   (d) 4.5 cm by 12 cm by 3.5 cm

2   The volume of each of these cuboids is 30 cm³.
   Find the missing lengths.
   (All dimensions are in cm.)

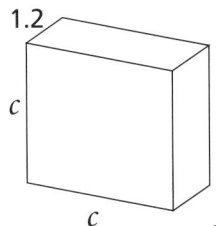

3 (a) A cube with sides 1 m long has a volume of 1 m³.
How many cm³ are there in 1 m³?

(b) 1 litre = 1000 cm³
How many litres are there in 1 m³?

(c) How many litres of water does this
swimming pool hold when full?

Section E

1 Here are some pictures
of prisms.
Each prism is made from
centimetre cubes or parts of them.

Work out the volume of each prism.

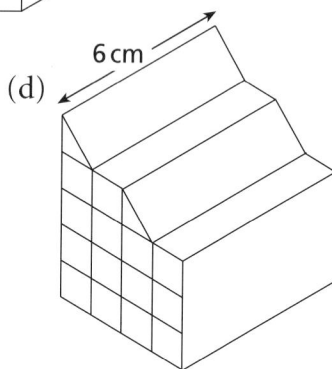

2 Calculate the
volume of each
of these prisms.

60

3 Calculate the volume of each of these triangular prisms.

(a)

8 cm 10 cm 6 cm 5 cm

(b)

2.8 cm 4.5 cm 2.5 cm 5 cm 4 cm 4 cm 5 cm

4 Calculate the volume of each of these prisms.

(a)

10 cm 7 cm 5 cm 6 cm

(b)

14 cm 10 cm 8 cm 5 cm 14 cm

5 A patio is made by pouring $10\,\text{m}^3$ of concrete to cover an area of $42\,\text{m}^2$ to the same depth all over.

What is the depth of the concrete, in cm (to the nearest cm)?

6 Each of these prisms has a volume of $60\,\text{cm}^3$.
Work out the missing dimensions.

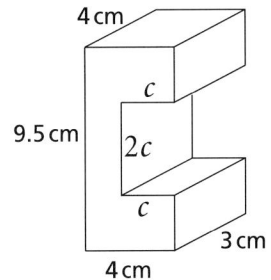

8 cm 6 cm a

b 3 cm 5 cm 2 cm

4 cm c 9.5 cm $2c$ c 4 cm 3 cm

Section F

1 This cube has a spot on the front and a spot on the back.
All the other faces are plain.

Copy and complete these nets of the cube.

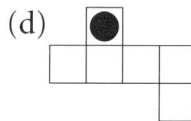

(a)   (b)   (c)   (d)

2 On a dice the numbers on opposite faces total 7.
Copy this net of a dice.
Find all the different ways of numbering the faces.

How many different dice are there?

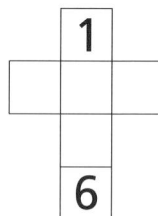

3 This cube has a square on three faces.
All the other faces are plain.

Which of these diagrams are nets of the cube?

A   B   C   D

E   F   G

62

4 The nets of these solids are incomplete.
   Sketch the incomplete nets and show the possible
   positions for the missing face.

   (a)

   (b)

   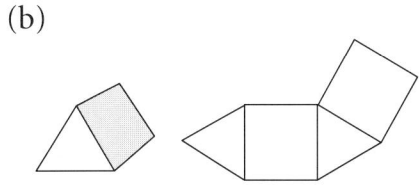

5 Here are the nets of some solids.
   Sketch the solids.

   (a)

   (b)

   (c)

   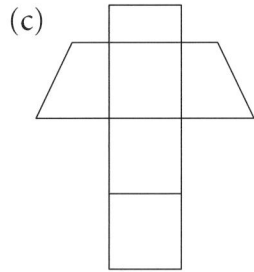

6 Each of these nets has one face missing.
   What shape is the missing face?

   (a)

   (b)

   (c)

   (d)

   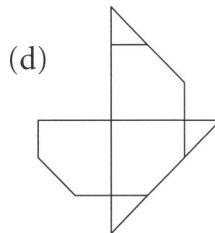

Section G

1 This is the net of a cuboid.

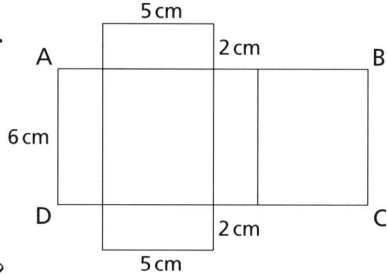

(a) What is the length AB?

(b) What is the area of rectangle ABCD?

(c) What is the surface area of the cuboid?

2 Find the surface area of each of these cuboids.

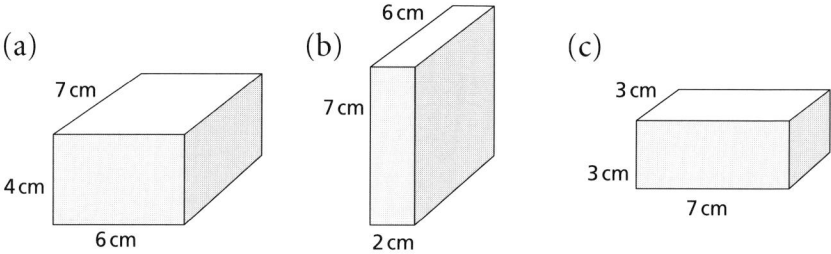

(a)

(b)

(c)

3 This solid …

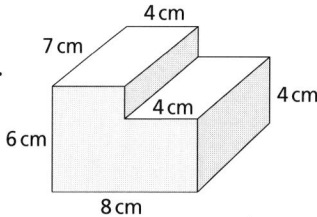

… has a net like this.

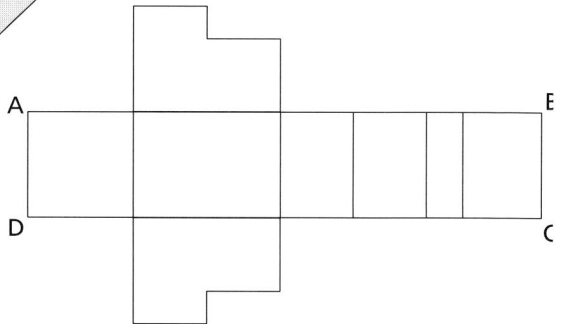

(a) What is the length AB?

(b) What is the length AD?

(c) What is the area of rectangle ABCD?

(d) What is the surface area of the solid?

64

4 Find the surface area of each of these solids.
All the measurements are in centimetres.

(a)

(b)

(c)
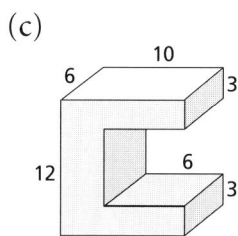

5 (a) What is the surface area of each of these cubes?

(i)

1 cm

(ii)

2 cm

(iii)
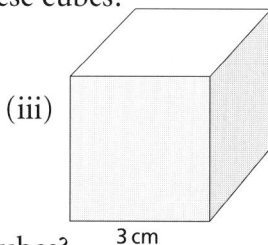
3 cm

(b) What is the volume of each of these cubes?

(c) What are the surface area and the volume of the next cube in the sequence?

(d) What are the surface area and volume of a 12 cm cube?

6 In each pair of cuboids below, the dimensions of the second cuboid are double those of the first.
Find the surface areas of each pair of cuboids. What do you notice?

(a) (i) 3 cm by 5 cm by 4 cm   (ii) 6 cm by 10 cm by 8 cm

(b) (i) 1 cm by 3 cm by 8 cm   (iii) 2 cm by 6 cm by 16 cm

7 In each pair of cuboids below, the dimensions of the second cuboid are three times those of the first.
Find the surface areas of each pair of cuboids. What do you notice?

(a) (i) 1 cm by 5 cm by 5 cm   (ii) 3 cm by 15 cm by 15 cm

(b) (i) 1 cm by 2 cm by 6 cm   (iii) 3 cm by 6 cm by 18 cm

22 Finding formulas

Sections A and B

1 These tables are arranged to form T-shapes.

Pattern 1   Pattern 2   Pattern 3

(a) Sketch patterns 4 and 5.

(b) Explain what pattern 10 would look like.

(c) Copy and complete this table.

Pattern number	1	2	3	4	5	10	100	n
Number of tables	4							

(d) One pattern has 16 tables. Which one is it?

2 These tables form O-shapes.

 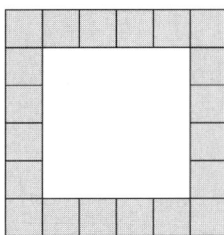

Pattern 4   Pattern 6

(a) Sketch pattern 3 and pattern 5.

(b) Explain what pattern 10 and pattern 20 would look like.

(c) Work out how many tables are in each pattern.
    Show your results in a table.

(d) Find a formula for the number of tables in the nth pattern.

(e) One pattern has 96 tables. Which one is it?

66

3 Here are some dot and line designs.
For each design

(i) sketch pattern 4

(ii) find a formula for the number of dots in pattern n

(a)

Pattern 1   Pattern 2   Pattern 3

(b)

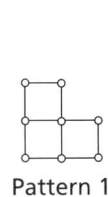

Pattern 1   Pattern 2   Pattern 3

(c)

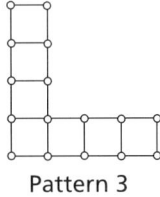

Pattern 1   Pattern 2   Pattern 3

4

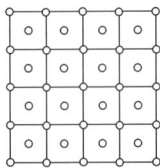

Pattern 3   Pattern 4

Find a formula for the number of dots in the nth pattern.

Sections C and D

1 For each of the following sequences:
   (i) describe a rule to go from one term to the next
   (ii) find the 10th term

   (a) 3, 6, 12, 24, 48, ...
   (b) 1, 5, 6, 11, 17, ...
   (c) 94, 96, 98, 100, 102, ...
   (d) 10, 11, 13, 16, 20, ...
   (e) 25, 23, 21, 19, 17, ...
   (f) 1, 2, 5, 14, 41, ...

2 Each of the expressions below gives the nth term of a sequence.
   For each one
   (i)   find the first eight terms of the sequence
   (ii) decide whether the sequence is linear
   (iii) work out the 50th term

   (a) $3n$
   (b) $n - 3$
   (c) $10 - n$
   (d) $n^2 + 5$
   (e) $2n + 4$
   (f) $\frac{42}{n}$

Section E

1   For each of the following linear sequences
    (i) find an expression for the nth term
    (ii) calculate the 100th term

    (a) 7, 10, 13, 16, 19, ...   (b) 7, 12, 17, 22, 27, ...
    (c) 3, 10, 17, 24, 31, ...   (d) 0, 5, 10, 15, 20, ...
    (e) ⁻1, 5, 11, 17, 23, ...   (f) 5, 5.75, 6.5, 7.25, 8, ...

2   For each of the following linear sequences:
    (i)   find the missing terms
    (ii) find an expression for the nth term
    (iii) calculate the 25th term

    (a) 9, __ , __ , 15, ...   (b) 2, __ , __ , 26, ...
    (c) ⁻1, __ , 5, __ , ...   (d) __ , 3, __ , 13, ...

3   I am a linear sequence. My 1st term is 7. My 5th term is 23.
    (a) Write down the 2nd, 3rd and 4th terms.
    (b) Find an expression for the nth term.

4   For the linear sequence 11, 15, 19, 23, ... , which term is 115?

5   Ben has £40 birthday money.
    Each week he adds £2.50 to his money
    so after 1 week he has saved £42.50.
    (a) How much will he have saved after 3 weeks?
    (b) Find an expression for the amount saved after n weeks.
    (c) How much money will he have saved after 15 weeks?
    (d) How many weeks will it take to save £100?

Section F

1   For each of the following linear sequences
    (i) find an expression for the nth term
    (ii) calculate the 20th term

    (a) 48, 46, 44, 42, 40, ...   (b) 20, 19, 18, 17, 16, ...
    (c) 100, 95, 90, 85, 80, ...   (d) 7, 4, 1, ‾2, ‾5, ...

2   For each of the following linear sequences:
    (i)   find the missing terms
    (ii) find an expression for the nth term
    (iii) calculate the 30th term.

    (a) 6, __ , __ , 0, ...   (b) 15, __ , __ , 12, ...
    (c) ‾2, __ , ‾8, __ , ...   (d) __ , 34, __ , 18 ...

3   For each of the following linear sequences
    (i) find an expression for the nth term
    (ii) calculate the 100th term

    (a) ‾3, 1, 5, 9, 13, ...   (b) 8, 7, 6, 5, 4, ...
    (c) 14, 18, 22, 26, 30, ...   (d) 10, 25, 40, 55, 70, ...
    (e) 8, 6, 4, 2, 0, ...   (f) 19.5, 19, 18.5, 18, 17.5, ...

㉓ Ratio

Section B

1   Most gold used for jewellery is a mixture of
    pure gold and other metals.
    18 carat gold is made by mixing 3 parts of
    pure gold with 1 part of other metals by weight.

    (a) How many grams of pure gold would you mix with:

     (i) 5 g of other metals   (ii) 12 g of other metals

    (b) How many grams of other metals would you mix with

     (i) 30 g of gold   (ii) 42 g of gold

2   Here is a recipe for 9 carat gold.
    Copy and complete the table.

    Mix 3 parts of pure gold
    with 5 parts of other metals.

Pure gold (g)	Other metals (g)
6	
12	
15	
	15
	30
	75

3   Here is the recipe for 22 carat gold.

    *Mix 33 parts of gold with 2 parts of silver
    and 1 part of copper by weight.*

    (a) How much silver and how much copper would you mix
        with 99 g of pure gold?

    (b) How much copper and how much gold would you mix
        with 20 g of silver?

    (c) How much gold and how much copper would you mix
        with 30 g of silver?

Section D

1   Amy made a necklace using 24 red beads and 18 green beads.
   (a) Write the ratio of red beads to green beads in its simplest form.
   (b) Write the ratio of green beads to red beads in its simplest form.

2   Write each of these ratios in its simplest form.
   (a) 4:6   (b) 12:4   (c) 15:25   (d) 15:6   (e) 21:18

3   Copy and complete these so that all the ratios in each group are equal.
   (a) 2:3   ☐:9   10:☐   (b) 4:1   ☐:3   8:☐
   (c) 6:2   ☐:1   18:☐   (d) 4:10   2:☐   ☐:15
   (e) 30:40   ☐:8   3:☐   (f) 7:3   21:☐   ☐:12

4   Match each ratio from group A with an equal ratio from group B.

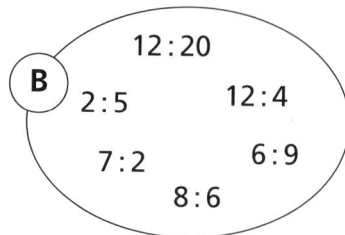

A: 20:30   21:6   9:3   3:5   8:20   12:9

B: 12:20   2:5   12:4   7:2   6:9   8:6

5   A compost for growing cacti is made by mixing loam and sand
   in the ratio of 3:1.
   (a) How many bags of loam go with 3 bags of sand?
   (b) How many bags of sand go with 12 bags of loam?
   (c) How many bags of loam and how many bags of sand are needed
       to make 20 bags of cacti compost?

6   Purple paint is made by mixing blue and red in the ratio of 3:2.
   (a) How many litres of red paint go with 6 litres of blue paint?
   (b) How many litres of blue paint go with 8 litres of red paint?
   (c) How many litres of blue paint and how many litres of red paint
       are needed to make 25 litres of purple paint?

Section E

1 Tony's class were going to raise some money for charity.
They decided to share it between two charities in the ratio of 2:3.

Write down how much each charity would receive if the class raised

(a) £10   (b) £25   (c) £80   (d) £42.50

2 Paul and Anna are being paid £30 to do some gardening.
They decide to share the payment according to
how many hours they work.

(a) How much is Anna's share if she
works for 2 hours and
Paul works for 4 hours?

(b) What is Paul's share if he
works for 2 hours and
Anna works for 3 hours?

(c) How much does they each get if
Paul works for 5 hours and
Anna works for 3 hours?

3 Bharat mixes blue and green paint in the ratio 5:4.
He likes the colour he gets and calls it 'murky green'.

How many litres of blue and how many of green will he
need to make these quantities of murky green?

(a) 36 litres   (b) 13.5 litres   (c) 17.1 litres

4 Share £120 in the ratio

(a) 1:2:3   (b) 2:1:2   (c) 2:3:5   (d) 2:3:7

5 Share £3.50 in the ratio

(a) 1:2:4   (b) 2:3:5   (c) 3:5:6   (d) 10:12:13

Section F

1   Each of these patterns continues in all directions.

What is the ratio of grey triangles to white triangles in each pattern?

(a)

(b)

(c)

(d)

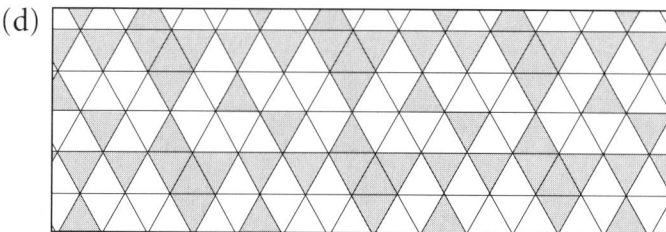

2   Using triangular dotty paper, design a tiling with grey and white tiles in the ratio $3:2$.

Section G

1   A shop sells two different writing sets.

    Set A contains 40 sheets of paper and 15 envelopes.

    Set B contains 25 sheets of paper and 9 envelopes.

    Which set has the higher ratio of sheets to envelopes?
    Explain how you decide.

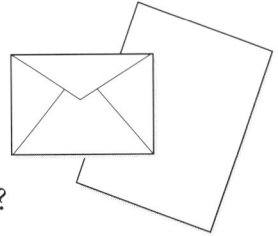

2   Different types of pastry use
    different amounts of flour and
    fat in their recipes.

    The table shows the flour and
    butter content for five pastries.

Pastry	Flour (g)	Butter (g)
Flan	100	75
Flaky	225	175
Rough puff	225	150
Choux	65	50
Puff	450	450

    Write the names of the pastries in
    order starting with the pastry with the highest ratio of flour to butter.

Section H

1   These rectangles are made by adding a square to the longest side
    of the previous rectangle.

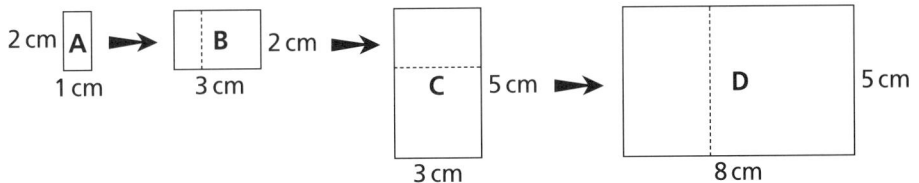

    (a) What are the sizes of the next three rectangles?

    (b) Calculate the ratio $\dfrac{\text{long side}}{\text{short side}}$ for each rectangle.

    (c) What do you notice about your answers?
        Investigate for more rectangles.

㉕ Functions and graphs

Section A

1 A swimming pool contains water to a depth of 80 cm.
A hose is turned on and the depth increases 20 cm in each minute.

   (a) Copy and complete this table showing the depth, d cm, after the hose has been on for t minutes.

t	0	1	2	3	4	5
d	80	100				

   (b) Find the formula connecting t and d. Write it in the form $d = ...$

   (c) Draw a graph from the table. Use the scales shown here.

   (d) Use the graph to find the value of t for which $d = 128$.

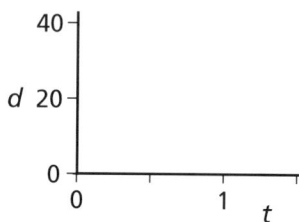

2 Mika has made a 'water clock'. It consists of a tall container with a tiny hole in the base, through which water leaks out slowly.

When she starts the clock, the depth of the water in the container is 30 cm.

The depth, d cm, of the water after t minutes is given by the formula $d = 30 - 4t$

   (a) Copy and complete this table.

t	0	1	2	3	4	5
d	30					

   (b) Draw a graph from the table. Label it '$d = 30 - 4t$'.

   (c) Use the graph to find after how many minutes the water is 16 cm deep.

76

Sections B and C

1   (a) Make a table of values for the function $y = 2x - 4$ for values of x from $^-4$ to 4.

    (b) Draw and label the graph of $y = 2x - 4$.

2   (a) Make a table of values for the function $y = 9 - 2x$ for values of x from $^-4$ to 4.

    (b) Draw and label the graph of $y = 9 - 2x$.

3   Find the equation of each line shown here.

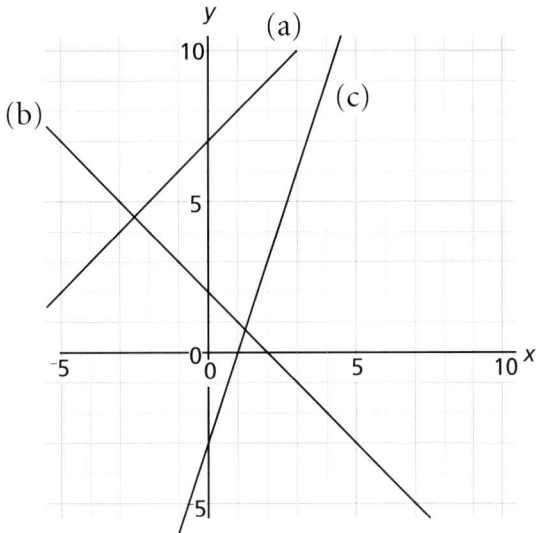

4   Sean did an experiment with a bed spring. He put different weights on it and measured its height.

He drew this graph of his results.

Find a formula linking h and w.

Mixed questions 3

1 ABCD is a cross-section of a motorway cutting.

(a) Calculate the area of the cross-section.

(b) The cutting is 120 m long and has the same cross-section along its length. Calculate the volume of earth that was removed when the cutting was made.

(c) The removed earth was carried away in lorries, each holding 82.5 m³. How many lorry loads were carried?

2 These objects are made by glueing 1 cm cubes together.

3 cubes

7 cubes

(a) Calculate the surface area of each of the objects shown above.

(b) Find a formula for the surface area of the object with n cubes.

(c) One of these objects has a surface area of 150 cm². How many cubes is it made from?

(d) This cross shape is made so that there are two cubes in each 'arm'.
Find a formula for the surface area of a cross shape with n cubes in each arm.

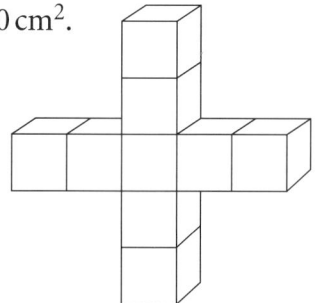

3 Ann is 3 years old, Brian is 4 and Charlie is 5.

  (a) Their aunt gives them £30 and they agree to share it in the ratio of their ages. How much does each of them get?

  (b) A year later, their aunt gives them another £30 and they have the same agreement. How much does each get this time?

4 Find a formula for the nth term of each of these linear sequences.

  (a) 2, 5, 8, 11, 14, 17, ...

  (b) ⁻7, ⁻3, 1, 5, 9, 13, ...

  (c) 26, 24, 22, 20, 18, ...

  (d) 5, ⁻4, ⁻13, ⁻22, ⁻27, ...

5 Find the equation of each of the graphs shown below.

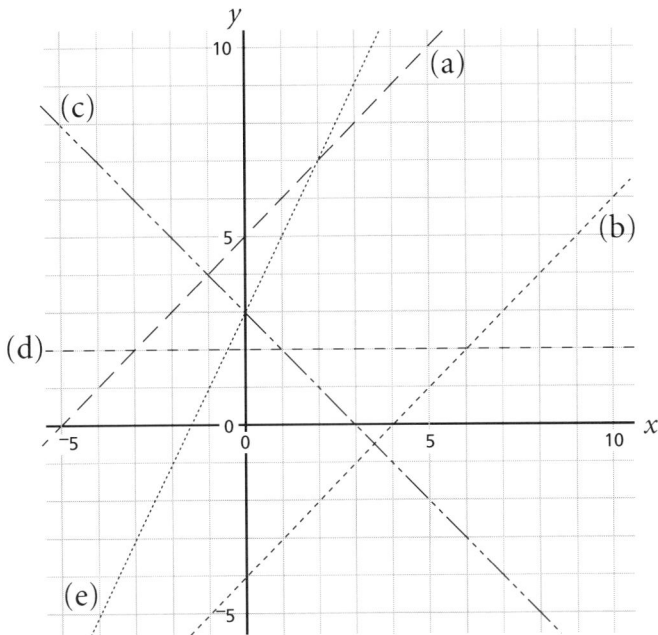

6 For each graph in question 5, work out the value of y when x is

  (i) 100

  (ii) ⁻100

7 Use a calculator to calculate (a) $\dfrac{8.05 - 1.85}{(4.7 - 3.2)^2}$ (b) $3.69 + \dfrac{\sqrt{1.69}}{5.2 \times 1.6}$

  Give your answers correct to two decimal places.

8 An metallic mixture is ... r, iron and tin in the ratio $3:4:5$ by w...

Calculate what perc...ge ... is copper.

9 Manoj counted the number of people (including the driver) in cars entering the town centre one morning.
Here is a summary of his results.

Number of people in car	1	2	3	4	5	6
Frequency	26	18	14	10	7	2

(a) Find the modal number of people in a car.

(b) Find the median number of people in a car.

(c) Find the mean number of people in a car, to two decimal places.

10 The 10th term of a linear sequence is 40.
The 3rd term is $^-16$.

Find   (a) the first term   (b) an expression for the nth term

11 Dawn has three pairs of gloves in her drawer, a red pair, a blue pair and a green pair.
Each pair consists of a left-hand and a right-hand glove.
The gloves are all mixed up and she takes out two gloves at random.

(a) Make a list of all the possible outcomes (for example, she could take the red left hand and the blue left hand).

(b) What is the probability that she takes out a left-hand and a right-hand glove?

(c) What is the probability that she takes out a pair of the same colour?

*12 Rajesh makes green paint by mixing blue and yellow in the ratio $1:3$.
Jane makes a lighter green by mixing blue and yellow in the ratio $1:4$.

Colin takes a litre of Rajesh's green paint and a litre of Jane's and mixes them together.
What is the ratio of blue to yellow in Colin's mixture?
(It is **not** $2:7$!)